• A HISTORY LOVER'S •
GUIDE TO THE
SOUTH SHORE

ZACHARY LAMOTHE

THE
History
PRESS

Published by The History Press
Charleston, SC
www.historypress.com

First published 2020

Manufactured in the United States

ISBN 9781467141345

Library of Congress Control Number: 2020930479

This book is dedicated to Tommy.

CONTENTS

ACKNOWLEDGEMENTS

This book would not have been possible without assistance from a variety of individuals. Throughout the planning, researching, writing, photographing and editing process, I have had immeasurable assistance along the way.

A thank-you to these individuals for help with the research: Julie Burrey of the Plymouth Public Library, Donna Curtin of Pilgrim Hall Museum, Angela Halstedt, Bob Harris at the Braintree Historical Society, Merlyn Liberty and Doug Ulwick of the Dyer Memorial Library, Brendan Kieran at the Massachusetts Historical Society, Enzo Monti at the Plymouth Cordage Company Museum, Amy Sheperdson at the Carver Public Library and Claire Spatola at the Hingham Historical Society

Thank you to these folks for their suggestions of historic places or attractions that I *must* include in these pages: Linda Arnold, Chris Arouca, Katie Burritt, Adam Coletti, Meaghan Fitzpatrick and James Hutchinson (thanks for joining for a research trip too!), Carlo Lamagna, David Lehan, David and Ann Marie Lyons, Matt Pomella, Mike Ruuska and Jen Worden.

This group took the time to (which is much appreciated) edit through their town's chapter: Carol Anderson of the Kingston Historical Society; James Baker, historian and museum curator (your knowledge of Plymouth is truly incredible); Wendy Bawabe and Caleb Estabrooks from the Norwell Historical Society; and Samantha Woods of the North and South Rivers Watershed Association.

Thanks to Adam Mannar, who on assignment took the photos of the National Monument to the Forefathers for this publication.

These individuals need an extra tip of the cap for helping on all ends of this project, including the research, editing and suggestion giving: Kezia Bacon, whose assistance was invaluable; Tom Begley, executive liaison for admission research and special programs at Plimoth Plantation; Lynne DeGiacomo at the Cohasset Historical Society; Bob Gallagher of the Scituate Historical Society; and Miles Prescott of the Pembroke Historical Society.

Of course, thanks to my mom, who edits everything I write (and has for the last thirty years), and my dad for just being there.

An outpouring of thanks to my wife, Jaclyn, who dealt with me throughout the whole writing process, even when the book's and our second son's due dates were within weeks of each other. (And she even took some photos for the book as well.) To my older son, Danny, who without (too much of) a fuss accompanied me to South Shore destinations near and far. And a special thanks to my editor, Mike Kinsella, for believing in this project.

INTRODUCTION

The South Shore of Massachusetts is constantly reinventing itself. It was the land of the Wampanoag and Massachusett tribes. Later, it was colonized by the English. A group of Separatists that eventually landed in Plymouth in 1620 settled the first permanent colony in New England. Soon, other colonies followed, such as Wessagusset (Weymouth) and Bare Cove (Hingham) to the north. During the seventeenth century, religion was an important part of the daily life of the citizens of the South Shore. Farming and fishing were vital. Some towns, such as Weymouth, Abington and Rockland, were highly industrialized. These three were important shoemaking towns. Others, such as Carver, Halifax and Pembroke, retained their rural feel. During the twentieth century, the major highway, Route 3, connected the South Shore to Boston. This helped the region grow dramatically. The northern towns of Weymouth and Braintree became bedroom communities of Boston. As the twentieth century progressed and Boston's allure grew even stronger, towns as far away as Plymouth and Kingston became part of the metropolitan Boston area, with a rise in population and suburban sprawl. The more things change, the more they stay the same, is the old adage. This rings true for the South Shore as well. In the twenty-first century, fishing remains important to the economy. Towns such as Hingham, Cohasset and Duxbury have kept the charm of a bygone era intact with quaint commercial centers and a small-town feel. Plymouth has become a destination not only for its history but also for its thriving downtown with independent businesses. Although the quest for religious freedom, a job in the shoe industry or the necessity to procure salt from the marshes are remnants of the past, the South Shore continues to be a major destination. From the fine sand beaches of Plymouth to the rocky coast of Cohasset, from the cranberry bogs of Carver to the streams full of herring in the springtime, the natural beauty of the region is topnotch.

Unlike well-defined regions such as the towns of Cape Cod, the neighborhoods of Boston or the municipalities that comprise Plymouth County, the South Shore is much more ambiguous. Some sources proclaim it as solely the coastal towns; others include farther inland. To the north, where does metropolitan Boston end and the South Shore begin? This collection includes all of the coastal towns and some farther inland such as Pembroke, Carver and Plympton. Quincy is the farthest north, and although the towns of Randolph and Holbrook were once part of Braintree, as was Quincy, the two first towns are not included, unless mentioned in reference to the historic Braintree.

Much of the history of the South Shore's towns overlap. This is due to a few reasons. For one, the area of land is not huge, meaning if cutting down trees for lumber was a major source of income in one town, chances are it was the same in the surrounding towns as well. Industries such as shipbuilding were not pigeonholed to one town. Instead, wherever there was an appropriate river, in this case the North River, shipyards sprang up, whether in Pembroke, Marshfield, Norwell, Hanover or Scituate. Another reason for overlap is because many South Shore municipalities broke away from the town of which they were originally a part.

The journey in writing this book has been fun. The idea of not only giving a glimpse into the towns' history but also providing attractions related to history has been rewarding.

1
PLYMOUTH

"AMERICA'S HOMETOWN"

No other place on the South Shore would be as fitting as Plymouth to begin our trek through history. While Plymouth is world renowned for being the permanent settlement of the group of Separatists from England that would be known to posterity as the Pilgrims, its history runs much deeper than that. From its earliest incarnation as a village of the Patuxet people, a group in the Wampanoag Nation, through its tenure as the Plymouth Colony, flourishing through subsequent centuries, Plymouth is a town that has had to constantly reshape itself to fit the desires of its inhabitants. Its Indigenous population utilized the abundant natural resources, including its fresh water, wild animals for food and a plentiful amount of fish in its streams and ocean. For the Pilgrims, Plymouth's steep hillsides, as well as its freshwater source, made a perfect location for a fort. Its proximity to water encouraged industry to thrive during the Industrial Revolution. In the modern day, oceanfront property, and with it, beaches and seafood shacks (along with historical tourism), bring the crowds. Whatever the decade, the area of land known as Plymouth has been utilized to benefit its inhabitants.

A perfect example of the ever-changing landscape would be Brewster Gardens and Town Brook. Today's serene walking path alongside a picturesque brook has gone through many iterations before its current status. Its earliest use was as the Nemassakeeset Trail, a path used by the Wampanoags to connect Patuxet to Nemasket (present-day Plymouth to Middleborough). The name *Wampanoag* refers to collective allied tribes in

The iconic Plymouth Rock. *Author's photo.*

the region. The source of fresh water in this brook and the adjacent springs led the Pilgrims to settle in the area. Later, the water was used for power, and as a result, much industry sprang up alongside it. An example of what early industry would have been like is the Jenney Grist Mill. Further manufacturing was located on the Town Pond and Brook into the twentieth century. Starting in 2002, a process of demolishing dams began so that the native river herring could reclaim their natural life cycle of swimming upstream from the ocean.

Although history books often begin with Plymouth as the landing place of the Pilgrims, its actual history goes back much further. The Patuxet people, who inhabited the area of modern-day Plymouth, were a subgroup of the Wampanoag tribe. Their lives revolved around their natural surroundings. In the more temperate months of the year, they lived in domed huts known as *wetus*. For food, they hunted deer, grew crops such as the three sisters (corn, beans and squash), hunted for whales, gathered seeds and berries, ate shellfish and fished the region's fresh and salt waters. They used leather for clothing. Unlike the European mentality, their belief was in communal land, not private. Their wetus were shrouded in chestnut or tulip poplar bark. They worked with wood and made tools as well. The language spoken was called Wopanaak or Natick; today, there is a movement to recover this language. The larger Wampanoag tribe ranged from eastern Massachusetts, including Cape Cod and the islands, to the Blackstone River and Newport, Rhode Island. The name *Wampanoag* means "People of the first light or the east." The tribe had many subgroups, including the Patuxet, Pokanoket, Mashpee and Titicut. Many of these words are still used today as place names. Sachems were the leaders, and the Great Sachem was known as a Massasoit. The Wampanoag believed in a balance in nature. This matrilineal society valued family and kinship. The Wampanoag society lasted for an estimated thirteen thousand years before the contact with Europeans.

By the time the *Mayflower* landed in Plymouth, around twenty European expeditions had visited Massachusetts, six recorded in the area of Plymouth. Plymouth, or Plimouth, first appeared on a map by Captain John Smith during his exploration in 1614. The places on his map were named by Prince Charles (the future King Charles I). The region had also been called Whitson Bay, Port du Cap St. Louis and Cranes Bay. A map by Frenchman Samuel de Champlain, who explored the Massachusetts coast from Gloucester down to the South Shore, helped in the navigation of the New World. He sketched a map of Plymouth, which included depictions of smoking wigwams. During Smith's visit in 1614, the meeting was initially hostile with the Native peoples of the region but soon gave way to friendly relations.

A British trader, Thomas Hunt, captured a Patuxet named Squanto, or Tisquantum, in 1614, who then spent time in England, Spain and Newfoundland. Hunt captured at least twenty Patuxet, presumably on Long Beach, who were then sold into slavery in Spain. Squanto was among those sold, but he was intercepted by Spanish friars. Afterward, he lived at the house of John Slany in England. Squanto met explorer Thomas Dermer in Newfoundland. Squanto, as an interpreter for Dermer, ventured back to the area of his origin in 1619 and found his village empty of souls. This region was once as occupied as the western part of Europe. The region's inhabitants had been plagued by a pestilence that claimed thousands of lives from Cape Cod to Maine. This was known as the Great Dying. The sickness was spread from contact with Europeans, and the Native Americans had no antibodies to fight the disease. This is known as virgin soil epidemic. The plague was rampant between the years of 1616 and 1619 in this area of New England. A theory is that it was actually a form of the bubonic plague, brought over from Europe. Upon arrival, the Pilgrims found cleared planting fields. The remaining villagers at Patuxet moved inward to the village of Nemasket. Intertribal warfare was common. The Wampanoag numbered around twelve thousand before the outbreak but were sizably reduced afterward. This played well for the Narragansett of Rhode Island, who did not feel the effects of the sickness. Only a few short years earlier, in 1605 when Champlain visited, the region was full of life.

If names such as *Mashpee, Massasoit* and *Samoset* have been embedded in the vernacular of the region, so have the last names of the first settlers, including *Alden, Howland* and *Bradford*. The Pilgrims' desire was to find a place where they would be allowed to worship freely. They felt that the Church of England was not representative of a true Christian church. The Pilgrims did not believe that the Church of England would ever be reformed to fit their beliefs. Among what they felt were the church's indiscretions were its pageantry, the role of priests, holidays and the act of kneeling to pray. The Separatists read the Geneva Bible and lived by it. Since in England they were a subversive sect, they had to congregate in secrecy. No official building was utilized; instead, they often met in homes at night. The influential minister Richard Clyfton gained a following, including the preteen William Bradford and William Brewster. A group of Separatists at Scrooby, England, attempted to leave for Amsterdam in 1607 and then travel to Leiden in Holland in 1608. The journey was plagued with misery, as the initial debarkation ended in disaster for many in 1607. They were supposed to board a secret ship, but in the end, they were betrayed and intercepted by the police, which led to the leaders being jailed and having their money stolen. The group, which had already sold almost all of the members' possessions, was nearly penniless. Another setback befell the Separatists in 1608, as some were captured before secretly boarding another ship. By 1609, most of the congregation had reached the Netherlands. English Separatists who formed their own parishes outside of the Church of England often left the country for the Netherlands due to acceptance by the Dutch. William Brewster, on his trips to the Netherlands, witnessed the freedom of religion there. The group felt that the state church had kept too many of the traditions of Roman Catholicism. Although they enjoyed the ability to practice their own religion in Amsterdam, they were not keen on the fact that groups they did not agree with, including Catholics and Jews, were also allowed to worship there.

After ten years or so, the Pilgrims needed a new place to call home. They felt that the native Dutch customs were becoming too ingrained in the lives of their children. William Brewster's publication of a book targeting the Church of England resulted in a warrant for his arrest, both in England and the Netherlands. He was stripped of his printing press and needed to leave, but the Netherlands was not far enough away. Although at odds with the Church of England, John Carver and Robert Cushman brokered a deal in

London with the Virginia Company. The Virginia Company advocated for the group to King James and other officials, as their proposed trip across the ocean would be a way to make economic gains for the corporation. In short, the deal would be that the group would work for the English corporation for seven years. Five days a week, the work that was done in the colony would benefit the company, which included the shipping of goods such as fish, furs and lumber back across the ocean, and two days of work would be for their own livelihoods. From the Netherlands, at Delfshaven, they sailed back to England on the ship the *Speedwell* to join with the *Mayflower*. The group departed from Southampton, England, on the *Mayflower* and *Speedwell*, but soon after embarkation, the *Speedwell* began to leak and had to turn around. On September 16, 1620, only the one-hundred-foot cargo ship, the *Mayflower*, set sail for the New World. The *Speedwell* did not make the journey. The travelers were hoping to disembark in the northern part of the Virginia Colony, which would be around today's New York City. (At this time, Virginia was practically the whole Eastern Seaboard.) This group was made up of not only Separatists but also people who were searching for a new life in the Virginia Colony whose motives were secular. After the grueling sixty-six-day journey, the land of Cape Cod was spotted. Plymouth would not be their first landing; this would be in Provincetown. They were not aiming to land in this region. Due to the lack of fresh water, they did not stay. A scouting party cast off in a smaller shallop boat led by Master Christopher Jones to explore for hospitable land. Winding down the coast of Cape Cod, they eventually landed on what they would name Clark's Island, named for the first of their party to set foot on the land. After two days on the island, including the Sabbath, the group sailed to mainland Plymouth. Eventually, Plymouth (Patuxet) was chosen due to its resources, most importantly, its freshwater source. When they landed in Plymouth, nowhere was there mention of stepping onto a certain rock. Plymouth Rock, as it is known today, is a symbol of America, but in reality, the significance of this object is more folklore than fact. The Pilgrims did not make note of the ground they landed on. They anchored the *Mayflower* within the harbor that is created by Long Beach. Just like the rock, the term *Pilgrim* was not used until the 1800s. Before that, they were called the "First Comers." After the *Mayflower*, the following three ships to bring more settlers from England were the *Fortune*, *Anne* and *Little James*.

After determining the most hospitable location to settle, the Pilgrims went ashore at Plymouth on December 18, 1620. The first winter of 1620–21 was arduous for the new settlers. Half of the original 102 passengers perished. Their bones were buried on the hillside known as Cole's Hill. Cole's Hill was discovered as an early burial place for the Pilgrims in 1854 when workers who were digging on the hill uncovered human remains. The early homes of Plymouth were built along what is today called Leyden Street. It is heralded as the oldest continuously used street in British North America. The street runs from the ocean to Burial Hill, which was the site of the first fort. From this vantage point, the Pilgrims could more easily defend themselves from attack, with a clear view of the ocean and the surrounding land.

Luck befell the Pilgrims on March 16, 1621, when Samoset, a Native American from the area of present-day Maine, wandered into the Pilgrims' camp and greeted them. Samoset had been visiting Massasoit when he approached the settlers and asked for a beer. He was clothed, fed and spent some time with the Pilgrims. Samoset clued the group into the important fact that a great epidemic had struck and claimed the lives of many people who lived here. The land that the Pilgrims settled was Patuxet. Meeting Samoset led to the Pilgrims being introduced to Squanto on March 22, 1621. Squanto taught the Pilgrims many skills that helped them adapt to the new land, including how to plant, hunt and fish. This fortuitous meeting was a primary reason for the colony's success. Through Squanto, the Pilgrims met Massasoit, the sachem of the Pokanokets, and a mutual alliance with the governor of Plymouth Colony, John Carver, was established. The official treaty was signed by nine other sachems on September 13, 1621. Squanto became an Indigenous ambassador to the Pilgrims. Through the Pilgrims' treaty with the Wampanoag, the two groups formed an alliance that would strengthen the tribe's power in the region against the rival Narragansett.

Massasoit sold off pieces of land to create towns, one of which is Bridgewater. Plymouth Colony grew and flourished, accommodating an increasing number of English settlers as the years progressed. Other villages founded around this time include Duxbury (1637) and Marshfield (1640). In 1621, the first wedding, that of Edward Winslow and Susanna White, took place in Plymouth. Immortalized in the nation's lore, the first Thanksgiving also took place that year. It was attended by Massasoit and around ninety of his brethren as well as fifty-three Pilgrims. Church services were on Sundays, and administrative meetings for the colony were held at the meetinghouse.

Ironically, although the Pilgrims wanted a place to call their own to worship freely, they did not accept any other religions or creeds. A historically significant dissenter was Roger Williams. In 1636, he left Plymouth due to intolerance and founded the Providence Plantation, which was the beginning of Rhode Island. The Pilgrims did not celebrate religious holidays in the traditional sense as they are thought of today. Sundays were steadfastly devoted to religion. There were also days of thanksgiving and of humiliation and fasting. The traditional Christmas feast of December 25 passed for the Pilgrims as any other day.

John Carver was the first governor of the Plymouth Colony upon arrival in 1620 until the spring of 1621. Although he survived the brutal winter of 1620–21, he died in April 1621. After toiling in the field on a hot day, he fell victim to excruciating pain in his head. It left him in a coma, with his demise coming days later. A few short weeks later, his wife joined him in death. Speculatively, Carver and his wife are buried on Cole's Hill, although this cannot be confirmed. William Bradford replaced Carver, and he was governor (not continuously) until his death in 1657. Bradford is famous for writing *Of Plimoth Plantation*, the most authoritative firsthand account of Pilgrim history. Myles Standish was another of the more well-renowned members of the group. He was not part of the Separatists but was hired as a military leader, a role he continued to fill upon his residence in Plymouth Colony. He would eventually settle in Duxbury. In 1643, Plymouth joined with Connecticut, Massachusetts Bay and New Haven as the Commonwealth of New England, and in 1692, the Plymouth Colony became part of the Massachusetts Bay Colony.

An unusual footnote to the Pilgrims' tenure in Plymouth was the arrival of pirates in May 1646. A Brit, Captain Cromwell, and his band of eighty pirates spent between a month and six weeks imbibing, consuming food and reveling in Plymouth. Inebriated privateers were arrested on occasion, but they were licensed by the English Crown. Bradford described them as madmen, who, even though they were put in prison and disciplined for heinous behavior, could hardly be kept under control.

Although the Plymouth Colony lasted for only seventy-two years, it made an indelible mark on history. Not only was it one of the earliest successful colonies in British North America, but its peace treaty made between the Wampanoag and Pilgrims was the only pact with the country's Indigenous population to not be broken. After its time in the limelight as "America's Hometown" (note—this phrase was not used until the mid-twentieth century), Plymouth as a community continued to grow and thrive. During the eighteenth century, much of the town was based on agriculture. It was rural, especially when compared to the more thriving Boston to the north, but its waterfront was bustling and its downtown had the beginnings of industry that blossomed fully in the nineteenth century.

Throughout America's involvement in wars, home and abroad, Plymothians have heeded their country's call to arms. One such story involves four men: freeman Cato Howe and three men who had been slaves at one time—Plato Turner, Quamony Quash and Prince Goodwin—all served in the Continental army during the American Revolution. Quash was still a slave until after his term as a soldier ended. Howe was stationed at Valley Forge during the treacherous winter of 1778–79. While in the army, he was part of the Second Massachusetts regiment. This troop saw action in major battles, including the Battle of Bunker Hill, and fought in the New York and New Jersey campaigns at battles such as Trenton, Princeton, Saratoga and Monmouth. Upon the four men's discharge, the Town of Plymouth granted ninety-four acres of land to Howe, where he and the others and their families settled. This area of town is known as Parting Ways and is close to the Kingston border. The land they settled was known as the New Guinea Settlement. Visitors can view the veterans' graves at Parting Ways Cemetery on Route 80, Plympton Road. Unfortunately, Plymouth was not immune to slavery; there were an estimated fifty slaves in town in the year 1740, with most being house servants.

Given Plymouth's well-situated harbor, its major industries were suited for the ocean. During the 1700s and 1800s, wharves lined the waterfront. Plymouth also played a part in the Industrial Revolution that blitzed through New England. With its prime oceanfront real estate, Plymouth's harbor morphed into a fishing, whaling and shipping destination. The shipyards began in the early years of the eighteenth century. Water Street was bustling with business, which, in addition to the wharves, included bakeries, blacksmith forges, storehouses, cooper's shops and sail lofts, where sails were made. With shipping and fishing such major industries in Plymouth, the town's merchants, workers and sailors were hit hard by the Embargo Act devised by President Thomas Jefferson in 1807. It disallowed the importation of foreign goods to the United States and banned the exportation of American goods. Plymouth residents banded together at town meetings and cried out for revocation of this act.

The coastline from North Street to around the area of Stephen's Field looked completely different than it does today. Plymouth Rock was located on Hedge's Wharf. Jackson's Wharf was built in 1750 near the end of North Street, but the construction of Long Wharf began in 1732. Hedge's was erected in 1749, and it was here boats brought to harbor such products as oil and iron and edible goods, including fish, oysters and corn. Other wharves that were situated on the coastline included Davis, Nelson's, Carver's, Robbins' and Barnes. The wharves' tenure in Plymouth came to a final conclusion with the Tercentenary Commission, which spearheaded the bulldozing of those remaining to reshape the harbor front to how we know it today.

Industry flourished in Plymouth along its waterways starting in the 1790s. Among the factories and mills here were the Robbins Cordage Company, which was bigger than the Plymouth Cordage Company initially. Even into the twentieth century, factories existed on the Town Brook and Town Pond, painting a much different picture than today. These included Plymouth Mills Iron Works, the Arthur Ellis and Sons Curtain Factory, the Godfrey Seamless Pocket Company and the E. and J.C. Barnes Company, among others. Plymouth's most famous mill complex opened in 1824. The Plymouth Cordage Company was heralded in the late 1800s and early 1900s as the globe's largest producer of rope and twine. One-seventh of the nation's rope used on ships was manufactured here. The factory became Plymouth's largest employer, and the village of North Plymouth grew up alongside it with the creation of row houses for factory workers. The Plymouth Cordage Company was founded by Bourne Spooner, William Lovering Jr., John Dodd and John Russell. The Cordage Company mills were constructed in North Plymouth. This section of town was known as "Plain Dealing" during the time of the Pilgrims and was later known as Bungtown, Seaside and also North Town before its current moniker of North Plymouth was popularized. In addition to the Plymouth Cordage Company, other smaller rope manufacturers or "ropewalks" were found throughout town, including off Howland Street and the area of Cold Spring Hill. With it also came various waves of immigration for factory work. With immigrants came the need for new institutions, most importantly, houses of worship. Plymouth's first Catholic church opened in 1874. By 1905, one quarter of the town's population were immigrants.

Other factories in town produced cloth, fiber, nails, anchors and metals. In addition to Town Brook, Nathan's Brook in North Plymouth, the Eel River and Wellingsley Brook were all sites of manufacturing. The Eel River powered a cotton mill, North Russell rolling and slitting mill and the Edes and Wood Zinc Company, among others. There was a woolen mill built in 1865, and there were cotton mills. For such a small body of water, Town Brook was the site of much industry. One factory, known as Bradford's Bedsteads, produced a metal hook that connected the headboard to the footboard of a bed, in the era before steel bed frames. This small metal hook led to a tremendously lucrative business. Downtown was booming. Ships were in the harbor, and industry was thriving, which led to an increase in population and business. To further expand on the productivity of an industrialized Plymouth and to complement the bustling wharves, the Old Colony Railroad opened on November 10, 1845. The railroad linked Boston to Plymouth. This railroad would eventually cover the South Shore, South Coast and beyond, extending to Fall River, Newport, Rhode Island, and Cape Cod, with lines traversing the whole region. Plymouth's population was 4,284 in 1820, but by 1905 it had grown substantially to 11,107. Plymouth's populace was also served by steamboat, connecting it to Boston. Easton, Massachusetts's shovel magnate, Oliver Ames Sr., lived on Summer Street, where his son Oliver Jr. was born. He would later expand his father's lucrative shovel company and become a prominent businessman and railroad president.

Plymouth's Training Green has had many uses throughout the years. It is one of the oldest parks in the country. Established in 1711, among its many purposes, the green was used for grazing cattle, as was Boston Common. (Cattle also grazed on Burial Hill.) Today, dog walkers and children utilizing the green's walkways for biking and grassy areas for sports are common sights. The Training Green has always been popular for recreational activities. Of course, the name refers to the local militia muster, which also took place here. On one corner of the green was a storage building for guns owned by the Plymouth Artillery Company, which was located there between the years 1820 and 1850. In the middle of the green is the Soldiers and Sailors Monument, which commemorates Plymouth's native sons who lost their lives in the Civil War. It was erected in 1869. This was also the site of a reservoir in the 1830s; it was used by the local fire company, whose first apparatus, a suction engine, was housed on Franklin Street. This fire engine, circa 1828, can be seen at the 1749 Court House Museum. The green has been used for many other functions, including art shows, temperance revivals and communal suppers. One of the most important events to grace the grounds of the green occurred on August 1, 1853. The occasion included a parade, fireworks display and dinner attended by two thousand people, which in turn led to the construction of the canopy over Plymouth Rock and the National Monument to the Forefathers. The present layout of the green can be attributed to the firm of famed landscape architect Frederick Law Olmsted, which designed the pathways that presently bisect the greenspace. The neighborhood that abuts the green is Watson's Hill. This, along with High Cliff (near the ocean closer to North Plymouth), are two notable locations of Native American burial grounds. Watson's Hill was where the first meeting of Massasoit and the Pilgrims took place and was the home of Hobomock, a warrior and translator.

The twentieth century brought major change to Plymouth in a variety of ways. The wharves that had marked the harbor for years were torn down, and the Main Street Extension was constructed. Main Street's former terminus was at Town Square at the intersection with Leyden Street (hence the name of this small stretch, Main Street Extension). A beautiful Baptist church with a prominent town clock was among the buildings lost to the creation of the street and bridge over Town Brook. With this and the tercentennial celebration, downtown Plymouth changed its landscape to cater to the new business in town, tourism. Much of what we know today as Pilgrim Memorial State Park was shaped during this era. The face of Plymouth's downtown was significantly altered in the mid-twentieth century as well. The area around Market, the foot of Summer, High Street and Spring Streets were bulldozed in the name of urban renewal. Around 120 homes and businesses were destroyed. In their place, new structures were built, including the John Carver Inn and the Spring Hill Apartments. Gone were the eighteenth- and nineteenth-century homes. Even the whole road of High Street was lost to history. Remnants of the style of building that was destroyed can be seen on Summer Street, but most of the structures were razed. The Town of Plymouth felt that these homes, which had been turned into tenement buildings, had fallen to the brink of condemnation, many irreparable. Once single-family homes on Summer Street had been turned into multifamily abodes. On High Street, houses that were kept up were staggered between those that were dilapidated. This was the pretense to demolish and rebuild, a product of the urban renewal craze that swept the nation in the mid-twentieth century. Although the layout of the downtown looks generally similar to today, some roads, such as High Street—which was a major component of the downtown—no longer exist. Others that were major thoroughfares are now simply access roads to larger streets. An example of this is Market Street. Today's Market Street links Main Street to Summer Street. Earlier, this was a major route. High Street extended from Market Street to Russell Street. What was High Street presently cuts through the Spring Hill Apartments as a walkway. From aerial maps, the former road can still be detected. Spring Street is now the walking path that slopes up to Burial Hill from Summer Street. Ironically, before it was lined with homes, it was a cattle path.

By the 1970s, the ever-present American suburban sprawl reached Plymouth, but unlike many communities, the big-box stores and fast food joints do not impede a visit to the downtown. Today's Plymouth has the unique distinction of being its own self-sufficient town with a thriving downtown and tourist-friendly waterfront. With its proximity to Boston, it has become a commuter town for city workers. The town is filled with history, which can be seen in many more locations than its museums alone.

From local beverage companies and restaurants to road signs and small businesses, the names of Plymouth's forefathers—European and Native American—are everywhere in town. From the John Alden General Store to Samoset Street, and from Myles Standish State Forest to Mayflower Brewing Company, the historical affiliations never end in Plymouth.

In addition to the thriving downtown, Plymouth's ninety-six and a half square miles of land encompass many varied neighborhoods, including West Plymouth (formerly known as Darby), North Plymouth, Manomet, Cedarville, South Plymouth and Chiltonville. The majority of its history is situated within the confines of the downtown, but other places of historical note in other areas of town will be discussed in a later section.

YOUR GUIDE TO HISTORY

HISTORICAL WALKING TOUR OF DOWNTOWN PLYMOUTH

The following tour encompasses many of the historic sites of Downtown Plymouth. The order is based on location, not by historical period or chronological order. Feel free to tweak this walk as you wish. It highlights many of the major historic sites. With a town like Plymouth, history can be found around every corner, so make this walk your own, add other places of note to it or skip ones that you have no interest in.

The walk begins on Summer Street at the Richard Sparrow House. Afterward, it traverses the Town Brook, stopping at many historic places along the way. It crosses over to Pilgrim Memorial State Park, continues up to the Mayflower Society House and Cole's Hill, travels to Leyden Street, up through Town Square and Burial Hill, and finally to Pilgrim Hall Museum. The walk is the perfect morning accompaniment to precede a visit to Pilgrim Hall.

Richard Sparrow House

42 Summer Street, Plymouth, MA 02360
508-747-1240, www.sparrowhouse.com

The Sparrow House is the oldest wooden structure in town. It's also one of the oldest houses in the state. Sparrow and his family arrived in Plymouth in 1633. The house consists of a small museum and gift shop. The museum shows life during this era, and its displays include a spinning wheel and kitchen table. There is informative signage on exhibits throughout. The gift shop showcases crafts, pottery and unique gifts. The Jenney Museum next door is also worth a visit.

Plimoth Grist Mill

6 Spring Lane, Plymouth, MA 02360
508-830-1124, www.plimoth.org, Admission $8

Just around the corner from the Sparrow House on Spring Lane is the Plimoth Grist Mill, formerly known as the Jenney Grist Mill. With all of the negative changes that happened with the urban renewal projects of the mid-twentieth century, the construction of this mill was a positive one, a re-creation of the 1636 gristmill built by John Jenney. Jenney and his family ventured to Plymouth in 1623 aboard the *Little James*. Jenney died in 1644, but after his death, his wife, Sarah, ran the mill. The mill met its final demise in 1847 when it was attached to the Robbins Ropewalk, as a fire engulfed the first industry in Plymouth. This reconstruction was built in 1970 and actually contains a millstone from Pennsylvania dating from the 1800s.

The gristmill is small but worth a peek inside. Corn is ground, as well as barley, wheat and rye. The tour starts on the top floor, where, on certain days, grinding can be witnessed. The millstone is quite impressive. For a history-related museum, there is a large STEM component, since hands-on milling can be seen. The bread baked at the Plimoth Bread Company (at Plimoth Plantation) originates here with grist used to make flour. Downstairs, observe the gears and the exhibits about its history. With its proximity to the native herring, the mill also presents a look into the ecology of the Town Brook. The mill also has a gift shop and pub, Lucioso's, on site. Cornmeal ground at the gristmill is available for purchase. The operating water wheel is neat, and the grounds are well manicured. Plimoth Plantation began operating the mill in 2012.

Town Brook

The one-and-a-half-mile Town Brook, which was the source of fresh water that helped the Pilgrims decide on Plymouth as their permanent settlement, flows through the Jenney Grist Mill. Wrap around the back side of the mill to continue the walk. This brook runs from Billington Sea, named for Pilgrim teenager Francis Billington who purportedly spotted what he thought to be an ocean. It is actually a large pond where kayak rentals are offered today. The Town Brook, from the harbor to Billington Sea, is also the location of a very active herring run every year in late April to early May. Watch the fish climb the ladder to get through the gristmill dam and look for the volunteers who count the fish as they shoot out of the fish ladder. The brook, along with the nearby springs, supplied the Pilgrims with their needed fresh water. Although it may seem unbelievable today, this brook was full of industry during the eighteenth and nineteenth centuries. Among the factories located here were Robbins Ropewalk, Standish Mills woolen mill and nail and tack manufacturers.

Brewster Gardens

30 Water Street, Plymouth, MA 02360

Continue on the path alongside the brook, walk under two underpasses and be welcomed to Brewster Gardens. This is below the lot of Elder William Brewster. As part of the rehabilitation of the waterfront, this park was created. The landscape was radically altered with the draining of the pond that was there and the filling in of land. Today, the park provides a serene backdrop for a walk, with paved and rock cobbled paths, along with a picturesque bridge over the Town Brook. There are benches to rest on along the way. The next few attractions are all within the confines of this park.

Pilgrim Maiden *Statue*

Inside Brewster Gardens

Walking over the bridge, turn left to see the *Pilgrim Maiden*. It was sculpted by Henry Hudson Kitson and dedicated in 1924 to commemorate the perseverance of English women in their new home. The bronze statue was ordered by the National Society of New England Women. The figure of the woman is not identified. She is young and dressed in traditional Pilgrim

The *Pilgrim Maiden* in Brewster Gardens. *Author's photo.*

garb and has tarnished into a greenish hue. She stands atop a rock, forever keeping watch on a small tranquil pond, a tributary of the Town Brook. She is tucked away at the west end of the park.

Immigrant Memorial

Inside Brewster Gardens

Walking from the *Pilgrim Maiden* toward the street, you will pass by another statue, a column with faces protruding from it. As the Pilgrims were immigrants to this land back in 1620, this stainless-steel piece commemorates the legacy of immigrants to Plymouth who settled here between the years 1700 and 2000. The sculpture, designed by Barney Zeitz, dates from 2001. An eagle adorns the top of the monument, and six faces and upper torsos of the town's immigrants who have made an indelible mark on Plymouth jut out of the statue's front.

Pilgrim Memorial State Park/William Bradford Statue

79 Water Street, Plymouth, MA 02360

Across the street from Brewster Gardens is the Pilgrim Memorial State Park. It provides gorgeous views of the harbor, and although close to the hustle and bustle of the waterfront, the feel of this park is more congruent with that of Brewster Gardens than of the crowded Town Wharf. It is hard to imagine while peering out into the serenity of the sea that it was only one hundred years ago that this area was lined with wharves and industry. This park is the focal point for annual festivals such as the Plymouth Waterfront Festival in August, the Fourth of July festivities and the Thanksgiving celebrations.

Along the edge of the park facing Water Street is a statue of Pilgrim William Bradford. Bradford became governor of the Plymouth Colony upon the death of John Carver. Between the years of 1621 and 1657, Bradford would serve as governor of the colony, although not continuously. He is best known for writing the definitive publication on Pilgrim life in Plymouth, *Of Plimoth Plantation*. The statue depicts Bradford in traditional Pilgrim attire with hat and cloak. This bronze figure was sculpted by Cyrus Dallin, who also designed that of Massasoit on Cole's Hill and *Appeal to the Great Spirit,* which is in front of Boston's Museum of Fine Arts. Although Dallin sculpted Bradford in the early 1920s, it was not installed until 1976.

Plymouth Rock

Inside Pilgrim Memorial State Park

It is hard to miss the elaborate columned structure that contains Plymouth Rock. This relatively small rock has a substantial place in history. Although the rock represents more oral tradition and possible folklore than absolute fact, it has its own nifty story. In the year 1741, Thomas Faunce brought to the forefront that a wharf had been built over the initial debarkation location of the Pilgrims. The site of the landing had been passed down to him via word of mouth. Before being nicknamed Plymouth Rock, it was known as Forefathers' Rock. A top piece of the rock broke off. The bottom stayed at the waterfront, while the top was displayed in the Town Square beneath a liberty pole and eventually moved to the Pilgrim Hall

Daylight fades over the Plymouth Rock portico. *Author's photo.*

Museum. The Pilgrim Society erected a canopy over the waterfront rock in 1859, and the two halves were made whole again in 1880. The canopy was designed by Hammett Billings and was located at Hedges Wharf. During this time, the rock was at ground level. Throughout its tenure of historical acclaim, onlookers literally wanted a "piece of the rock" and used tools to chip away at it. In 1920, as part of the tercentennial celebration, its current portico and position on the sand were created. It was designed by famed architects McKim, Mead and White, the firm that also built the Boston Public Library, Pennsylvania Station and the Brooklyn Museum in New York City.

Mayflower II

Pilgrim Memorial State Park pier, Plymouth, MA 02360
508-456-1622, www.plimoth.org, Admission charged

No, the original *Mayflower* did not survive Father Time. This replica of the ship the Pilgrims sailed on can be toured, with actors aboard who may discuss certain aspects of the boat and who are there to answer your questions. The boat, along with the Plimoth Grist Mill, is operated by Plimoth Plantation, and a combination ticket is available for purchase (along with the plantation museum). The ship was built in England in the mid-1950s by Warwick Charlton's Project Mayflower Ltd. The *Mayflower II* sailed from Plymouth in Devon, England, to New England, recreating the journey of the Pilgrims before arriving at its permanent home in Plymouth Harbor. The *Mayflower II* was designed by noted nautical architect William Avery Baker and was part of the original vision of Plimoth Plantation founder Henry Hornblower II. Both groups in the United States and England concurrently had ideas to build such a ship. The English group read an article that the museum was planning to construct the boat, and thus, the collaboration between Plimoth Plantation and Project Mayflower was created. The replica has sailed into many ports of call, including Providence, Boston, Fairhaven and Mystic, Connecticut, where it was restored in recent years at Mystic Seaport Museum. The ship draws visitors to the Plymouth waterfront even if they do not visit the museum; it is one of the highlights of the town.

Pilgrim Mother *Statue*

72 Water Street, Plymouth, MA 02360

Walk across Water Street from the ship, but head back south, the way you came, to continue the tour. The *Pilgrim Mother* is located on the right-hand side of the road. Built for the tercentennial celebration but given by the Daughters of the American Revolution in 1925, this statue is a fountain with a Pilgrim mother standing underneath the fountainhead. It is in honor of the women of the *Mayflower*. It was created by C. Paul Jennewein, a German sculptor, who also has works featured at the Philadelphia Museum of Art, the White House and Rockefeller Center.

Mayflower Society House

4 Winslow Street, Plymouth, MA 02360
508-746-2590, www.themayflowersociety.org, Admission $7

A quick walk uphill from the *Pilgrim Mother* statue on North Street is the Mayflower Society House, built circa 1754. (It's technically on Winslow Street.) This is the headquarters of the General Society of Mayflower Descendants, an exclusive group that includes only those individuals who

Peering through the garden at the Mayflower Society House. *Author's photo.*

have actual evidence of being a direct relative of a *Mayflower* passenger. The eighteenth-century home is stunning, painted a stately white and accented with black shutters. Many of the features of this home, including the porches, cupola and wings, were added by former owner Charles Willoughby. This was the home of Edward Winslow, who was the great-grandson of Edward Winslow, a Pilgrim. The home has held various uses over the years and was even the site of Ralph Waldo Emerson's second nuptials. Tours are available of the home, and there is a research library on site. Make sure to stroll through the gardens in the back of the home for Plymouth's finest hidden garden—it is a true gem.

Spooner House

27 North Street, Plymouth, MA 02360
508-746-0012, www.plymouthantiquariansociety.org, Admission $6

Cross the street at the Mayflower Society House and walk up North Street until you reach the Spooner House on your left. Run by the Plymouth Antiquarian Society, this house depicts what life was like for a family in Plymouth during the 1700s. Although named for the Spooners, who lived in the house for roughly two hundred years, the first occupant was Hannah Jackson. The first Spooner to call this house home was the Deacon Ephraim Spooner, who was a merchant. Through the next two centuries, generations of Spooners lived within these walls. Their wares are on display as if the family had simply left for the afternoon. The house was deeded to the Plymouth Antiquarian Society for historic preservation in the 1950s. The Antiquarian Society itself has a unique history. It was founded in 1919 by a group of women who felt that preservation of historic property was a worthy cause to advocate for at a time when they were not yet allowed to vote, as a response to the Hedge House's pending demolition.

Three additional houses are not on the route but are all worthwhile stops while visiting historic Plymouth. In addition to this property, the Antiquarian Society is also in possession of the 1677 Harlow Old Fort House, whose building materials include pieces of the fort that the Pilgrims initially erected. It is located at 119 Sandwich Street. The society also runs the 1809 Hedge House with its octagonal rooms at 129 Water Street. Tours are offered at both of these historic homes. This home was moved to its current location, as it used to stand where Memorial Hall does today.

Another historic home of note is the Jabez Howland House, run by the Pilgrim John Howland Society. It still offers a glimpse into a seventeenth-century home, as the oldest parts of it date from 1667. It is located at 33 Sandwich Street.

Massasoit Statue

35 Carver Street, Plymouth, MA 02360

Back on our route, head east from the Spooner House (toward the waterfront) on North Street, but bear right onto Carver Street (the road parallels Water Street but is on top of the hill). The next few sites are all located at the top of this hill. Cyrus Dallin, the same man who sculpted William Bradford, was the creator of this imposing figure. In contrast to the size of Bradford, Massasoit stands at a larger than life, ten feet tall. He proudly gazes into Plymouth Harbor. This statue was commissioned in 1921 for the tercentennial. The National Day of Mourning Thanksgiving protest takes place in front of this statue yearly.

Cole's Hill Burial Ground/Sarcophagus

Carver Street, Plymouth, MA 02360

The hill in front of you is Cole's Hill, the first burial ground that the Pilgrims used. Unmarked, the remains went unnoticed until the 1700s. Events throughout the next two centuries uncovered human bones. In 1735, a rainstorm created a deluge that unearthed buried human remains. The Pilgrims who did not survive the first winter were buried here. Among the interred was first governor John Carver. In 1855, workers digging a trench uncovered the remains of a man and a woman who were speculated to be John Carver and his wife. More skeletal artifacts were unearthed that year and put into the canopy placed over Plymouth Rock. In the late nineteenth century, when more remains were discovered, some members of the public took some as keepsakes. On the top of the hill is a sarcophagus, built in 1921, which houses the bones that were interred below the canopy. Cole's Ordinary was on Carver Street.

Leyden Street

The oldest street in British North America in continuous use is Leyden Street. Carver Street wraps around to join with it. This was the site of the earliest settlers' houses, the actual Plymouth Plantation. Leyden is named for their former place of residence in the Netherlands, Leiden.

Town Square

Leyden Street leads out to Town Square. The center of the village is surrounded by three public buildings, two churches (the National Pilgrim Memorial Meetinghouse and the Church of the Pilgrimage) and the 1749 Court House Museum. (At Christmastime, the square is decorated by a gigantic evergreen.) The National Pilgrim Memorial Meetinghouse, until recently known as the First Parish Plymouth Meetinghouse, is the original church of the Pilgrims. The original house of worship for the parish was at the fort, behind the current building on Burial Hill. The church was recently purchased by the Mayflower Society. The 1899 church is the fifth meetinghouse to sit on this site. The congregation originated in Scrooby, England, in 1606, and the Pilgrims reestablished it in Plymouth in 1620. It's the oldest parish in New England. The windows on the church are beautiful Tiffany stained glass and tell the story of the Pilgrims. Town Square was the center of civic and community life for the Pilgrims. These two churches are in direct lineage from the original church of the Pilgrims at Scrooby but separated in 1801.

1749 Court House Museum

1 Town Square, Plymouth, MA 02360
508-830-4075, Admission, free

On the south side (left-hand side) of Town Square is the 1749 Court House Museum. This museum is free. It has a small but interesting collection of artifacts, including the town's first fire engine, a hearse and artifacts from the New Guinea settlement at Parting Ways. It is the oldest wooden courthouse in America and was used by the Town of Plymouth as the seat of government until the 1950s. It was converted into a museum in 1970. It is truly a gem of a museum, small, but with fantastic displays and information. There are objects and information from the recent archaeological digs performed close to Burial Hill at the location of the former palisades of the original settlement, on the side of today's School Street. There is an exhibit depicting the urban renewal project that drastically altered Plymouth during the 1960s. The before and after pictures are fascinating.

Burial Hill

School Street, Plymouth, MA 02360

Looming behind Town Square is Burial Hill, which, along with the graves of many notable early residents, includes the finest view in town. There is no question why the Pilgrims chose this location for the site of their fort. From atop this hill, the vantage point is unmatched. The ocean views stretch out past Long Beach, where they could witness any incoming ship. Although the fort is gone, a place marker shows where it once was. In addition to its use as a fort, it was used as a church and meetinghouse in the early days of the Pilgrims. In Plimoth Plantation's re-creation of Leyden Street, a replica of the fort can be visited. At Plimoth Plantation, the colonial settlement is enclosed by a high wall; unfortunately, tangible remnants of the wall no longer exist. There are three main entrances to the cemetery: one right behind the First Parish church, a pathway that skirts alongside the John Carver Inn (the former Spring Hill Lane) and one off South Russell Street (at this one, there is parking).

Among the notable interments are that of Pilgrims John Howland, William Brewster and William Bradford. The earliest settlers were buried at Cole's Hill. Mary Allerton was laid to rest here near the Cushman obelisk. She was the last of the original Pilgrim settlers to die, in 1699, as she was only a small child during the passage to America. Bradford's gravestone is an imposing marble obelisk. He died in 1659, and the exact location of his burial is undetermined. Edward Gray's gravestone has the distinction of being the oldest on the hill, circa 1681. Legend marks Howland as the first to be enshrined in the hill's earth in 1672 (his gravestone is much newer), but it is speculated that others were buried earlier. Patriots James Warren and his wife, fellow revolutionary and writer Mercy Otis Warren, are also buried here.

Pilgrim Hall Museum

75 Court Street, Plymouth, MA 02360
508-746-1620, www.pilgrimhall.org, Admission $12

After entering the cemetery behind Town Square, exit it at South Russell Street (diagonally across from the recently refurbished town hall, which was the 1820 courthouse). Near the public restrooms at the town hall, stop to look at the map of Plymouth from 1882 to see how the town has changed and developed. Walk South Russell and take a left (head north) on Court Street. After a few blocks, the Pilgrim Hall Museum, the final stop on the tour, is on the right-hand side.

On Court Street is the Pilgrim Hall Museum, which features artifacts from the Pilgrims as well as rotating exhibits. The museum is two floors and is manageable to explore, even with children. Pilgrim Hall was built by the Pilgrim Society (which was founded in 1820) in 1824 and claims to be the oldest public museum in constant operation in the country. The collection includes Governor Bradford's chair, John Carver's sword, paintings and other possessions of the Pilgrims. The building itself has expanded throughout the years, adding a library wing in 1904 and extended in 2008. It had a bas-relief situated in its pediment, where the fanlight is placed today. The facade, adorned with six Doric columns, was designed by McKim, Mead and White in 1922. Its collection includes a fine assortment of paintings, furniture, period artifacts and detailed exhibits that depict all aspects of the history of the Pilgrims.

The journey of historic downtown Plymouth ends here, but there is much more history to see in town, although it may be easier to access the rest via car. (Addresses are provided, and many are still walkable from downtown.)

ADDITIONAL DOWNTOWN ATTRACTIONS

National Monument to the Forefathers

Allerton Street, Plymouth, MA 02360

Tucked out of the way, but still in walking distance of downtown is the National Monument to the Forefathers on Allerton Street. It is said to be the largest granite statue in the world at eighty-one feet. From the harbor, the top of the statue can be seen rising above the tree line and the surrounding buildings. It was completed in 1889 in tribute to the Pilgrims, their contributions and their lasting influence on the ideals of America. The focal point is the figure of Faith who stands tall, pointing her finger to the sky, flanked by seated granite human embodiments of Education, Law, Liberty and Morality, representing the ideals of the forefathers and of America. Embedded within the stone benches on which the figures sit are smaller ones of Prophet, Evangelist, Justice, Truth, Tyranny Overthrown, Peace, Youth and Wisdom. The quote etched onto its side was written by William Bradford. Its sheer size is quite impressive; it can be walked or driven around and is free.

America's Hometown Trolley

Tickets available at kiosk near Plymouth Rock and Plymouth Waterfront Visitors Center 508-746-0378, www.p-b.com/plymouth-trolley-tours, Admission $15 (all-day pass)

During the warmer months, the Plymouth and Brockton Street Railway Company operates open-air trolley tours to the downtown's tourist attractions and historic sites, including Plimoth Plantation, Plymouth Rock and the National Monument to the Forefathers. Riders can hop on and off all day and are given a schedule of the trolley's arrival times. These trolleys can also be rented out for special occasions. Lively trolley drivers and tour guides provide interesting historical tidbits as the trolley glides through town. The company itself, now mainly affording bus service in the region, has its own interesting history. It was originally founded as the Plymouth and Kingston Street Railway, which provided streetcars for local travelers in the late 1800s and into the 1900s. In 1899, the Plymouth and Brockton Street Railway absorbed the Plymouth and Kingston railway. Ridership decreased over the early twentieth century, as cars replaced streetcars for many. Buses run by the Plymouth and Brockton Company replaced the streetcars in 1928. Ironically, some of the routes that the streetcars used to serve are now traveled on by the company's open-air trolley.

The Plymouth Yacht Club

34 Union Street, Plymouth, MA 02360
Not accessible to the public

Although a private club, the building that houses the yacht club (and has since 1929) and adjacent Doten's Wharf was once the Doten lumberyard, begun by Samuel Doten in 1825. The club bought the building from the Atwood Lumber Company in 1929. The two-story wood-paneled club offers gorgeous views of the harbor. It has a bar and function facility. Inscribed on the wall of the club's first floor are the signatures of former lumberyard workers. The yacht club itself has a long history dating to its charter in 1890.

OUTSIDE OF DOWNTOWN

Although many of the town's top historical and tourist attractions are located within the walkable town center, Plymouth is Massachusetts's largest town area wise, and other sections of it have places of historic importance to visit. Unlike the more well-known downtown, some of these are located more off the beaten path—some of which may even be a surprise to the locals.

Plimoth Plantation

137 Warren Avenue, Plymouth, MA 02360
508-746-1622, www.plimoth.org, Admission $30

For many visitors to Plymouth, Plimoth Plantation is their destination. Deservedly so, it is one of the premier living history museums in the nation. Step into the seventeenth century to view the daily life of the English colonists and Wampanoag people. The English village is a re-creation of the original Plymouth Plantation located at Leyden Street and Town Square. Along with replica homes, there is a fort overlooking the village and farm animals. Try talking to the actors about something modern, and they will look puzzled, as they do not break character. Adjacent to the Pilgrim settlement is the Wampanoag Homesite, also from the seventeenth century. The men and women here have knowledge of the present as well as the past, which presents a different experience from the English Village, although they still work on traditional crafts and meal preparation. Even children are seen playing period games. There are extensive research facilities on-site, as well as a highly regarded farmer's market on Thursdays and a cinema that shows first-run independent films in the evenings. At the village, rare animals can be seen, including San Clemente Island goats, milking Devon cattle and Wiltshire horned sheep. These can be seen up close in the Nye Barn.

Plimoth Plantation was incorporated in 1947, opening to visitors a year later. The museum was originally located on the waterfront, in the area where today's two Plimoth Plantation buildings are (the waterfront gift shops). Even a replica of the Pilgrims' original fort, similar to the one located at the museum today, was on the waterfront, on the opposite side of Plymouth Rock. One of the two houses still at the waterfront dates from 1955. The museum lasted around ten years at this site. The land that houses

Plimoth Plantation is the premier site for historical tourism in the South Shore. *Jaclyn Lamothe.*

the museum today belonged to the family of Plimoth Plantation founder Henry Hornblower II. He summered on this estate, which belonged to his grandmother and had been in the family since 1898. Once she passed, the estate became the Eel River campus of Plimoth Plantation, which opened in the late 1950s. Hornblower's mission was to create a museum based on experience, not one of solely observing artifacts under glass. Plimoth Plantation consists of reproductions, not primary objects like the Pilgrim Hall Museum, but it tells the history of the lives of the men, women and children of Plymouth. In the English Village, there are various ways to interpret the past: first person, with the costumed actors in seventeenth-century garb, who, when asked, would not know the answer to a question about the year 1630; as well as third person, with modern guides dressed in twenty-first century attire to offer a current perspective on the past. At the Wampanoag Homesite, there are non-Native guides along with people dressed in traditional seventeenth-century Native clothing who speak to guests from a twenty-first century perspective, sharing not only the history of the people of Southern New England in the 1600s but also their experiences as Native people today. Signage throughout enriches the visit with additional information.

Tom Begley, executive liaison for administration, research and special projects, recommends visiting the Wampanoag Homesite first, then the English Village, which depicts the natural progression of Plymouth through history. He highly touts both the *Mayflower II* and the Plimoth Grist Mill as must-sees as well. The experience at Plimoth Plantation varies based on the time of year, where certain festivals such as the Green Corn Festival or Thanksgiving are celebrated. A new addition to the museum is a *wetu* (Wampanoag word for house) built outside of the English Village, which depicts a typical site post-English contact.

More than just bringing awareness to the true story of the Pilgrims and Wampanoags, Plimoth Plantation has a large presence in town. Begley describes Plimoth Plantation as the "hearth of the community," as it has become a gathering place for Plymotheans for a variety of activities. Along with the farmer's market, Plimoth Plantation holds many community events, including the annual heirloom plant sale, Living Proof Spirits Tasting (a festival of craft spirits) and Harvest Dinner. It is a popular site for celebrations such as weddings and other special events. For more information on Plimoth Plantation, the *Mayflower II* or the Plimoth Grist Mill visit www.plimoth.org.

Billington Sea

Accessed via Morton Park at Morton Park Road, Plymouth, MA 02360

Walking from Brewster Gardens west past the gristmill, follow the Town Brook to eventually reach Billington Sea. History books tell the story of Francis Billington, who was a teenager when he arrived in Plymouth on the *Mayflower* and is said to have climbed a tree atop a hill and spotted a body of water he thought was the Pacific Ocean. Billington and one other passenger went to explore the area but were put off when they spotted traces of a Native American settlement and headed back. Billington's father, John, was put to death for murdering another settler, John Newcomen. Just a tad smaller than the Pacific, Billington Sea is 269 acres in size, with an average depth of only eleven feet.

Cordage Park/Plymouth Cordage Company Museum

36 Cordage Park Circle, Plymouth, MA 02360
508-747-4271, www.plymouthcordageco.org, Admission free

The largest employer in Plymouth during its heyday, the Plymouth Cordage Company was world renowned, as it was the largest rope and twine manufacturer on the planet. Chrysler's new economical car, the Plymouth, was named for the twine's use in the bailing process. Founded in 1824 by Bourne Spooner, the wooden quarter-mile ropewalk building was the first from the company. The rope was constructed by hand. This building was moved in 1950, as it had lain dormant for years after the rope-making process had become mechanized and was transported to the Mystic Seaport Museum. When the USS *Constitution* was refitted in the 1920s, it was done with Plymouth cordage. Twine and rope were made for ships, for bailing, even for lassos used by cowboys, among numerous things. Once rope's heyday was over, the company concentrated on twine. There was a sister factory in Welland, Ontario. The Plymouth Cordage Company was much more than solely a place to work, though. As the campus grew, so did the facilities. Harris Hall, a restaurant, was on site. Cordage had its own library, which had many books written in German, Portuguese and Italian, the three major nationalities of the immigrants who came to work in the factory. It fielded its own baseball team, had a clinic and offered classrooms,

The Cordage Company was the largest employer in Plymouth. *Author's photo.*

a sportsman's club and, of course, homes. Constructed in 1885, the brick mill, which is the focal point today, was where twine was made. It is still in wonderful shape, and its current use is as an office building with satellite college campuses and a few restaurants and a winery. The rest of the former campus is currently in the process of rehabilitation with a condominium complex built adjacent to it. After World War II, the company's extracurricular activities and benefits decreased as the call for higher wages replaced peripheral benefits. It officially closed in 1970, although it had been downsizing steadily through the 1960s. Visit the one-room Plymouth Cordage Company Museum located in the main entrance. It is full of pictures and artifacts from the company's history. The staff is knowledgeable and friendly and admission is free, but the museum is open only from noon to 4:00 p.m. on Saturdays and Sundays.

Enisketomp

Located at the service plaza off of Route 3 South

Traveling down Route 3 South, have you ever noticed the large statue outside the McDonald's at the service plaza? Most drivers do but do not know the backstory of it. The statue of a Native American is part of the Trail of Whispering Giants, all created by sculptor Peter "Wolf" Toth. *Enisketomp* means "human being" in Wampanoag, and according to the plaque at its base, the statue is a gift to the people of Massachusetts. Toth began sculpting these larger-than-life figures in 1972, with the *Enisketomp* completed in 1983. He is carved of red oak. Toth's seventy-four (as of 2018) figures can be seen in all fifty states as well as one in his native Hungary. (Due to weather or neglect, not all seventy-four are still in existence.) It took Toth, who typically uses primitive tools on his sculptures, about three months to complete *Enisketomp*. His idea was to promote a consciousness to the plight of the country's Indigenous peoples. The statues range from twenty to forty feet in height. For his creation of *Enisketomp*, he met with and studied the Wampanoag to make sure every detail was historically correct. The tall, relatively thin sculpture's focal point is its face. It is a wise face, but one that has seen much hardship in the past. *Enisketomp* is located at the service plaza off of Exit 5 on Route 3.

RECREATION AND NATURAL ATTRACTIONS

Long Beach

1 Ryder Way, Plymouth, MA 02360

Three-mile Long Beach juts into the ocean at the confluence of the Eel River. The shoal forms a natural barrier that protects (along with Saquish) Plymouth Harbor from rough seas or, in days gone by, unwanted visitors.

The beach has its own storied past. From the accounts of Portuguese explorer Estêvão Gomes (who sailed for Spain) in 1525, a map of the northeast coast of America included Plymouth Beach. It was also on the famous map by Samuel de Champlain from his voyage into Plymouth Bay in 1605. In 1614, Thomas Hunt captured at least twenty Patuxet, including Squanto, presumably from Long Beach, where they were playing a game. Historically, the beach has been a source of sustenance from its birds, fish and seaweed. In the late nineteenth century, the beach was the site of a hotel with entertainment and dining. This was destroyed in November 1898 along with all but one cottage on the peninsula. Serious storms through the present day have damaged Long Beach. These include the hurricane of 1635, hurricane of 1938, various gales and storms up through March 2018. Seawalls and dikes have been placed to keep the structure and shape of the beach to prevent the complete destruction of it.

Gurnet and Saquish

Accessed via Duxbury Beach, private

Gurnet and Saquish are peninsulas that protect Plymouth Harbor. Its shape is reminiscent of a backward *L*. Unlike Long Beach, which is populated by a handful of houses, these peninsulas have a larger concentration of homes. Gurnet and Saquish have been connected by land since the eighteenth century but were once separated by water. Although technically part of Plymouth, the only way to access them is through Duxbury Beach. The white lighthouse with black trim, the Plymouth or Gurnet Lighthouse, is located at the tip of the land. The lighthouse itself has an interesting history. The first lighthouse here was constructed in 1768. It was destroyed by fire in 1801 and rebuilt two years later as two separate twin lighthouses. It was rebuilt again in 1842. The more northern of the two twin lights was dismantled in 1924. Nearby, built in 1776, was the Gurnet Fort, later known as Fort Andrew, erected to protect the harbor during the American Revolution. (Fort Andrew no longer stands.) The worst shipwreck, that of the *General Arnold*, occurred near Saquish in the harbor. The vessel was stranded in a snowstorm, and before it could be rescued, seventy-two of the one-hundred-person crew froze to death. The Plymouth Light was the first set of twin lights in the country. Hannah Thomas, lightkeeper when her husband, John, died of smallpox in 1776, was the first female light keeper in the nation.

Clark's Island

If the shape of Saquish resembles Italy, then Clark's Island would be its Sicily. It is named for one of the pilots of the *Mayflower*, John Clark. It is he who is said to be the first of the crew to have disembarked on the island. The group of Pilgrims sent from the *Mayflower* to explore the area of Patuxet first stayed on Clark's Island. Local Native Americans were held on Clark's Island for a year during King Philip's War. There are annual trips out to the island, but overall this is privately owned.

White Horse Beach

Off of Taylor Avenue, Plymouth, MA 02360

One of the most picturesque beaches in New England can be found in the Manomet section of Plymouth. White Horse Beach has fine, soft sand without the abundance of rocks that plague many of the South Shore's beaches. The slightly curved coastline is perfect for beach walking, and the expansiveness makes White Horse a winner for a day at the beach. Like many seaside towns, its character has changed over the years. Where there were once vacation amenities such as hotels and a bowling alley, now the neighborhood is primarily residential. Some homes are seasonal, and others are occupied year-round. Parking is limited, which keeps the beach less crowded. There is a small lot for town beach stickers. White Horse Rock, more commonly known as Flag Rock, has a neat bit of lore that surrounds it. The rock, offshore about a quarter of a mile, is adorned with a painted American flag that gets touched up once it becomes too faded. In 1940, the rock was graffitied with a swastika. A group of teenagers, led by the Dreary brothers, took it upon themselves to paint an American flag over the swastika. Previously, there was an attempt to clean off the swastika, but to no avail. The young people took red, white and black paint (they had no blue paint) and turned what was once a horrendous eyesore into a point of village pride and patriotism. All of the brothers enlisted in the service after the attack on Pearl Harbor, with one even losing his life in World War II. Legend says that it may have been Germans who graffitied the rock, as U-boats were known to be cruising the waters off the New England coast during that time. Plymouth is known far and wide for its Fourth of July festivities. Not to compete with the town center, Manomet's celebration takes place on July 3 and includes the burning of large bonfires, a tradition since the nineteenth century.

The Pinehills

33 Summerhouse Drive, Plymouth, MA 02360
888-209-8880, www.pinehills.com

Historically, the area of the Pine Hills of Plymouth is hilly terrain located south of Chiltonville. The Pinehills is a planned created village nestled into the woods around Clark, Beaver Dam and Old Sandwich Roads. Nearby on Old Sandwich Road (primarily a dirt road, heralded as the oldest continuously publicly used road in the United States) is Rye Tavern. The tavern, which dates from 1792, built by Josiah Cornish, is a Cape Cod cottage. Its inviting décor warms up a cold winter night. In summer, the outside bar is a lovely setting for dinner and a drink. Much of the fresh produce is grown in the on-site garden. Its use as a tavern is nothing new, and as the road was a major thoroughfare, the building has had previous incarnations as inns and taverns. Located within the confines of the Pinehills is Sacrifice Rock, whose name certainly conjures up gory images. Old Sandwich Road was used as a

Welcome to the Pinehills.
Author's photo.

path for the Wampanoag. Along this path, a harmless token of sacrifice was often left. Branches, for instance, would be left to allow the spirits to make the traveler's journey a safe one. Sacrifice Rock is managed by the Plymouth Antiquarian Society and had a large significance to the local Indigenous people. It is located at 286–296 Old Sandwich Road.

Cleft Rock

Park entrance at 290 State Street, Plymouth, MA 02360

Cleft Rock in the Pine Hills section of Plymouth is a unique rock formation. It looks similar to a train tunnel or a table. It looks as if a flat rock had been placed on top of one that has been split (or cleft). Legend says that Native Americans used this rock as a watchtower to keep eyes on Cape Cod Bay. The rock's formation is large, roughly twenty-five feet by twenty-five feet.

Fresh Pond Preserve

220 Bartlett Road, Plymouth, MA 02360

Fresh Pond is located in the Manomet section of Plymouth. Fishing and boating are popular here. Also located on the banks of the pond is a Native American burial ground.

Parting Ways Cemetery

Plympton Road, Plymouth, MA 02360

Due to Cato Howe's service in the American Revolution, the Town of Plymouth granted him land in 1792. He asked three other African American men and their families, also from Plymouth, to join him in creating a settlement. These men, who were also veterans of the Revolution, were Quamany Quash, Plato Turner and Prince Goodwin. (Quash was not freed until his military tour of duty was over.) They settled the ninety-four-acre New Guinea Settlement. (This was a common name for African American enclaves.) It is located on today's Route 80, near the border with Kingston. Their gravesite is visible at the Parting Ways Cemetery, which is on the land that was granted to them by the Town of Plymouth. There is a trail in the woods as part of this National Historic Landmark. Howe lived here until 1824. As the years went on, the settlement eventually included a transient population that held no title to the property. The last descendant, James Burr, lived here until 1908. The name "Parting Ways" comes from the fact that the road is on the way out of Plymouth, where it leads to Carver and Plympton separately. Artifacts of the settlement can be seen at the 1749 Court House Museum.

Chiltonville

The Chiltonville section of Plymouth is located south of downtown, encompassing Plimoth Plantation. It is a classic picturesque New England village with its white steeple and Colonial houses. The horse farms on Old Sandwich Road, Sandwich Road and Jordan Road feel more like Kentucky than southeastern Massachusetts. Bramhall's Country Store is a quaint general store that serves lobster rolls and ice cream in the summer. It has been a general store since 1828, but the building dates to 1750. It is located at 2 Sandwich Road in the heart of Chiltonville.

Bramhall's country store, serving Chiltonville since 1828. *Jaclyn Lamothe.*

Eel River Preserve and Russell Mill Pond Preserve

204 Long Pond Road, Plymouth, MA 02360, Admission free

In 2011, the Town of Plymouth completed the restructuring of the Eel River, historically known as Finney's Meadow. The river, which winds its way through the preserve, was once used to power mills and was redirected for cranberry farming. The reservation reclaimed forty acres of a former cranberry bog. Through its efforts, the town was awarded the Coastal America Partnership Award. The two preserves are connected by a pedestrian footbridge, which is the location of a former dam. The two loop walks are relatively short and are both accessible off Long Pond Road. There is a parking lot for the western section (about two miles in length), at the corner of Long Pond and Boot Pond Roads and also down the driveway of the Southeastern Massachusetts Pine Barrens Association. Many of Plymouth's preserves are not well publicized and require some searching to find. The scenic trails abut the Eel River and Russell Mills Pond. With the founding of the preserve, seventeen thousand Atlantic white cedars were planted—the largest concentration of the trees in the state. The trails also connect with other departments' trails and are very close to Myles Standish State Park. A goal of local conservationists is to be able to walk from Myles Standish to Pilgrim Memorial State Park all via trail. On the Russell Mill Pond trail, the path is marked by arrows, but it can be slightly confusing. Also, the path, which skirts closer to the shoreline, is steep with unstable footing. Along the trail is an old decrepit cabin that has been completely vandalized and strewn with graffiti. The Eel River was important for providing a staple of the Pilgrims' diet, the eel. The preservation has given shelter to the endangered red-bellied cooter turtle as well as a variety of fish, plants and reptiles.

Myles Standish State Forest

East entrance off of Long Pond Road, Plymouth, MA 02360; Admission free

The largest area of protected land on the South Shore, Myles Standish State Forest is about the size of Providence, Rhode Island. The forest was purchased by the State of Massachusetts in 1916; at over fifteen thousand acres, it is easy to get lost, even by car. Recreational activities abound, such as swimming at one of the many ponds, camping and hiking the many miles of trails, biking and horseback riding. The park is an example of a pine barren ecosystem with scrub oak and pitch pine growing naturally. There is also an array of feathered, aquatic and reptilian species. The forest is located both in Plymouth and Carver. The main entrance is off Long Pond Road in Plymouth. (Note—do not be surprised to see signs for "MASAC at Plymouth," as there is a substance abuse center buried deep inside the forest, which is understandably off-limits to the public.)

Ellisville Harbor State Park

1861 State Road, Plymouth, MA 02360, Admission free

Plymouth is so large that driving to Ellisville State Park from downtown feels like traveling through a few towns. Look for the state park sign, and pull into the driveway. The state acquired the property in 1991. The hike travels through wooded groves with its culminating feature being the rocky barrier beach. The trail steadily winds down to sea level. It is a secluded gem in the preservation land of the South Shore.

Center Hill Preserve

Center Hill Road, Plymouth, MA 02360, Admission free

Located close to Ellisville Harbor at 158 Center Hill Road, this nature walk is one of the finest for young children. It is separated into two parts, crossed by Center Hill Road. The western portion is a walk through the forest, and the eastern section's path travels through shady woodlands but soon exits onto a beach. The beachside walk is the best for children since it is very short. Young children will feel a sense of accomplishment in making the journey, where older ones may want more of a challenge. This rocky and sandy outcropping, similar to Ellisville, is serene and a lovely change from crowded, more popular beaches. Ellisville is the more well known of the two parks; typically, Center Hill is sparsely populated, even in the height of summer. The swath of beach accessible from the preserve is expansive. Look for basking seals at Ellisville and Center Hill's beaches in the summer.

2

WEYMOUTH

LABORARE EST VINCERE: "TO WORK IS TO CONQUER"

Every school kid knows that Plymouth was the first colony in New England, as well as one of the first in America, and Plymouth was the first town established in Massachusetts. No one gives a thought to the second though. Unknown to most, the second-most senior town in the commonwealth is Weymouth.

Weymouth was established only two years after Plymouth, in the year 1622, although this settlement, known as Wessagusset, was not long lasting. (The word *Wessagusset* is even written on the town symbol.) Weymouth is in proximity to Boston, about 12 miles south of the city, and is 21.6 square miles in size. Given the town's geographical nearness to Boston, from the mid-twentieth century to the present it has been a bedroom town of the city. Unlike most South Shore towns that established a definite town center, from larger communities such as Plymouth to much smaller ones such as Halifax, Weymouth grew around four different community squares. While many of the South Shore communities' borders have been shaped and reshaped time and again, Weymouth's have remained steadfast since the seventeenth century, even though its neighbors have changed names (such as Rockland having been formed out of Abington). For a relatively small town geographically, Weymouth shares its borders with many others, including Braintree, Quincy, Holbrook, Rockland, Abington and Hingham.

Weymouth's history is multifaceted, running the gamut from agriculture to heavy industry. Ships, blimps and shoes were all manufactured in town.

Evening looms in Weymouth. *Author's photo.*

Each square had its own identity based on the industry at hand. For instance, Jackson Square was influenced by the Weymouth Iron Works, located close by. Weymouth's most famous resident was Abigail Adams, first lady and close adviser to her husband, John. From factory work to fishing fleets and its colonial past to suburban sprawl, Weymouth's history is long and winding and has been shaped by many forces.

The land that became Weymouth was inhabited by the Massachusett tribe. Upon settlement, a deal was brokered with Chickatawbut, sachem of the Massachusett, for the land to start the colony. Many of the major roads in Weymouth were paths used by the local Native Americans. Originally settled in 1622 as Wessagusset, the eventual settlement was spearheaded and financed by Englishman Thomas Weston, who also backed the Pilgrims' voyage. This time though, he was interested in another settlement based on monetary motives unrelated to religion. Weston envisioned that a colony could establish a network of trade between the settlement and England in which goods such as lumber, furs and fish were traded. The geographic location was chosen ahead of time. Weston's group aboard the fishing boat the *Sparrow* numbered sixty, and they settled in the area known as North

Weymouth. The settlement location was near King's Cove and Great Hill, upriver from where Weymouth Fore River meets the sea. Similar to their English brethren to the south in Plymouth, the settlers at Weymouth were not faring well. Unlike Plymouth, there was no change in their fortunes, however. Rough weather conditions and a short supply of victuals made matters worse. The group reached out to Plymouth for assistance, but their pleas were dismissed since the Pilgrim group could not spare provisions needed for themselves.

A year later, in 1623, tensions rose between the settlers and the Native Americans. There was speculation that the local Indigenous people were planning a raid on Wessagusset with intent to kill, followed by an attack at Plymouth. Word was sent to the military leader of the Plymouth Colony, Myles Standish. He and eight others struck against the Massachusett, killing warrior Pecksuot. After this skirmish, the colony effectively disbanded, with most residents fleeing south to Plymouth and later returning to England and a handful of others migrating to Maine. Later that year though, another group was scheduled to arrive at the Wessagusset Colony. This group was led by Robert Gorges, who brought over 120 men, women and children with him. Among the group was William Blackstone, who would eventually settle Boston. Of the new arrivals, some became permanent residents, while others sailed back to England. This group settled at Hunt's Hill, close to Wessagusset.

Geographically speaking, Weymouth, or Wessagusset, was a prime spot to call home. It had a naturally protected harbor due to the peninsula of Hull protruding into the Atlantic Ocean, as well as the numerous Boston Harbor Islands blocking a direct route into the harbor. The area had plentiful freshwater sources, including the Weymouth Back and Fore Rivers, as well as ponds including Whitman's and Weymouth Great Pond. The second attempt at settlement was permanent. During the 1630s, the settlement became part of the larger Massachusetts Bay Colony, and by 1635 the name was officially changed to Weymouth, after its namesake in England. That year, twenty-one more families arrived, including that of the Reverend Joseph Hill from Weymouth, England. This was the year that Weymouth was officially granted town status. Town meetings decided the community's affairs. The first church in Weymouth doubled as the meetinghouse and a fortress, common for the time. Eventually, in 1721, a second meetinghouse was granted in South Weymouth at Columbian Square. This became the Second Precinct of Weymouth. The new meetinghouse was met with disapproval from the residents of the northern section of Weymouth, as townspeople thought the cost was too high to erect a new building and employ another minister. The third church, the Union Congregational Church, followed in 1810 in Weymouth Landing. During the American Revolution, Weymouth was the site of the Grape Island Alarm. Grape Island is one of the harbor islands, located just off the coast from Weymouth Neck. A local militia chased off British soldiers who were obtaining supplies at the island. The colonial force was shooting toward the island, but by the time they were able to approach Grape Island by sea, the British had fled.

As the town of Weymouth grew, so did the variety of commercial enterprises. Citizens became traders, merchants and builders. Other villages such as South Weymouth—the site of future mills—began to sprout up. Weymouth Landing, being situated on the water, was a shipbuilding hub in the late seventeenth century. Weymouth, similar to many South Shore industrial towns, was a center for shoemaking. The first shoe shop was started by James Tirrell in 1808 on Front Street. His products were sent off to Boston and then shipped to New Orleans. As Tirrell needed more room for a larger operation, the second site of his factory was located at Independence Square in South Weymouth. Shoe factories became a major employer in Weymouth; 73 percent of the town's workforce was employed in the shoe industry. The last and one of the most well known was Stetson Shoe Company, which operated from the early 1880s until 1973. Another industrial force in Weymouth was iron production. The facility was located near Whitman's Pond. It began in 1837 and ended in 1885. Bog iron was discovered in the town near Great Pond, which led to the boom of nail production. The Weymouth Iron Works was a sprawling complex that employed a large number of workers. It consisted of thirty buildings and canals, dams and a wharf. Iron production ceased in 1885, the same year the large Stetson Shoe factory opened its doors on Main Street. This building has been beautifully rehabilitated into medical offices as Stetson Place. The shoes produced here were of the finest quality. When Weymouth's largest shoe factory opened, its iron industry came to a trickle. The first cobblers did not have a permanent shop; instead, they were nomads. Permanent shoe manufacturing in Weymouth began in small shops known as "ten footers," most often located in the back of a cobbler's house. There were many other successful manufacturing companies in Weymouth. E.S. Hunt and Sons produced fireworks and hand fans. Granite and slate were mined from quarries in town.

River herring was a source of nutrition, a natural fertilizer and a symbol of pride. Among early industries, including procurement of salt from the marshes, fishing was important in Weymouth. The river herring seasonally ran a course from the Atlantic to Whitman's Pond through the Weymouth Back River. Once upon a time, 100,000 fish were taken in one day. Along with the natural world, industry was prevalent in this section of Weymouth from the early days of its settlement. As early as 1724, a passage for the fish was needed to complete their yearly migration. Jackson Square and the nearby pond would become the site of the sprawling Weymouth Iron Works. The industrial site actually declared fish rights in 1845. A modern passageway for the fish was designed in the mid-twentieth century, but it has been updated and revamped since.

Given its proximity to Boston, Weymouth was connected to the capital city by rail beginning with the advent of the Old Colony Railroad in 1845, which traveled through the southern part of town. Four years later, the South Shore Railroad rumbled through the coastal route as it passed through Weymouth heading toward Braintree or Cohasset. In the late 1800s, trolleys and streetcars began to shuttle passengers around town. Buses now follow many of the same routes as the former streetcars. The Old Colony Railroad (eventually the South Shore Railroad was obtained by the OCR) was revived once again, as the Massachusetts Bay Transit Authority's commuter rail extended to the South Shore on the former track.

Steamships also connected the harbor town to the city and places beyond. Streetcars lined Weymouth's major roads and connected it to nearby towns. A staple of industry in Weymouth was the Bradley Fertilizer Plant, the largest of its kind in the world. This factory complex began operations in the early 1860s and lasted well into the twentieth century. It was situated on Weymouth Neck/Fort Point area. Today, this land is covered with high-rise condominiums and the Webb Memorial State Park

The four distinct areas of Weymouth that were settled are Columbian Square in South Weymouth, Bicknell Square in North Weymouth, Jackson Square in East Weymouth and Weymouth Landing, which is on the coast, near the border with Braintree and Quincy. Historically, North Weymouth was known as Old Spain, where corn, wheat and grain were grown and processed. The origin of the moniker of Old Spain has been lost to the sands of time. North Weymouth, given its proximity to the sea, was used as a summer resort area. The Lovell's Corner neighborhood was an early area for amusement but was soon eclipsed by nearby Paragon Park in Hull.

During the twentieth century, especially after World War II, Weymouth boomed. Given the spread-out nature of the town geographically, the automobile linked square to square as well as provided means to travel outside of town. Couple this with the construction of Route 3 in the 1960s, and Weymouth's population bubbled at roughly 55,000 in 1970, which is only slightly less than the 56,667 citizens tallied at the 2017 census. That is a stark contrast to many South Shore towns that were relatively rural until the latter part of the twentieth century and are still dramatically expanding. Through the modernization of Weymouth, much of its history has been obscured by mini-malls and shopping plazas. Looking at the ornate brick Weymouth Town Hall, one may feel a bit of déjà vu. This is because as a tribute to the town's extensive history the municipal building was constructed in 1928 as a replica of the Old State House in Boston. The South Shore Hospital opened in 1922 and has expanded tremendously through the 1900s and 2000s. It has become the premier hospital on the South Shore.

Military facilities throughout the twentieth century had a major role in Weymouth. In addition to a Nike missile site, at South Weymouth, a large U.S. Navy facility was constructed in 1942. Blimps were built here to spy on Nazi U-boat operations under the high seas. The largest blimp hangar in the world was at Naval Air Station South Weymouth. NAS South Weymouth was one of the biggest facilities of its kind during World War II. It was reopened in 1953 as a training station and eventually closed for good in 1997. Since then, it has gone through a series of redevelopments, including its current incarnation as Union Point. Union Point is a mix of residential neighborhoods and commercial enterprises with an emphasis on greenspace and walking paths. The idea is that Union Point will become a futuristic "smart city." At almost 1,500 acres of developable land, the former naval base is prime real estate in an area of the country that has been settled by Europeans since the 1600s and where land is at a premium. During the twenty-first century, Weymouth has found itself at a crossroads of self-sufficient community and bedroom town to Boston. While much of the former manufacturing has come to a close and many residents are employed in Boston, Weymouth still retains a community feel. It has fine parks such as Webb Memorial and Abigail Adams State Park, opened in 2003, on the waterfront. Weymouth also has a burgeoning craft brewery scene with Barrel House Z, Article XV and Vitamin Sea brewing companies.

Barrels greet visitors to the Barrel House Z brewery. *Author's photo.*

Hidden in plain view are houses reflective of important architectural styles of American history. Early homes, such as Abigail Adams's birthplace, are in the Cape Cod style. Federal and Georgian styles followed, as did Greek and Gothic Revival architecture. These were popular in conjunction with the mid-1800s Industrial Revolution. The Victorian era saw homes in popular styles such as the French Second Empire, Queen Anne and Richardsonian Romanesque, the latter as demonstrated by the Fogg Opera House in Columbian Square. The Fogg Library is another example of Weymouth's beautiful architecture. The 1897 stone building is designed in the Renaissance Revival style. Twentieth-century architectural styles are predominant too, with classical and Colonial Revival homes and of course the bungalow and raised ranch. These styles would have been too cookie cutter for progressive architect Frank Lloyd Wright, who spent the early years of his childhood in Weymouth.

Additionally, Weymouth's military background is vast. It is written about in detail in the chapter on the South Shore's military history.

YOUR GUIDE TO HISTORY

Abigail Adams Birthplace

180 Norton Street, North Weymouth, MA 02191
www.abigailadamsbirthplace.com, Admission $5

Abigail Smith Adams is arguably Weymouth's most famous resident, and her birthplace has been moved twice. Her father was the minister of the First Parish Church in Weymouth. Adams is best known as the first lady of President John Adams and the mother of President John Quincy Adams. She was born in 1744. Her birthplace dates from 1685 and was the parsonage for the church. It was located at the corner of East and North Streets. The home was moved to Bicknell Square, where it became a boardinghouse for workers on a farm. By 1838, prospects for the home were low. It was readied for the wrecking ball. At this time, the Abigail Adams Historical Society jumped in and lobbied to save the home. The Town of Weymouth let the society purchase a plot of land for one dollar only three hundred feet away from its initial location. The house was split into halves and carried to its present location at 180 Norton Street.

The Civil War Memorial watches over the North Weymouth Cemetery. *Author's photo.*

The home is still operated by the Abigail Adams Historical Society. The home is a museum dedicated to the life of Adams and is full of period furnishings. It is impeccably well preserved after being on the brink of demolition in the 1830s. It is open in the warmer months on various days. Check the website for up-to-date information.

North Cemetery

126 Norton Street, North Weymouth, MA 02191

This sprawling cemetery, with sloping hillsides offering glimpses of the ocean, dates from 1636, the year of the first recorded burial. It is serene, with a museum or park-like atmosphere. The cemetery is split in two by North Street as it heads north toward Weymouth's earliest English settlement. Notable interments include that of Abigail Adams's parents, Reverend William Smith and Elizabeth Quincy Smith. Also buried here is Thomas Watson, assistant of Alexander Graham Bell and recipient of the first words ever transmitted by telephone. Bell's command, "Mr. Watson, come here, I want to see you," has been immortalized for posterity. Watson was successful in his own right; he went on to establish the Fore River Shipyard in nearby Quincy. His gravesite overlooks his beloved shipyard. The headless skeleton of Pecksuot, the Massachusett warrior killed by Myles Standish and company, is said to be interred here. It was unearthed during the construction of a nearby home. High atop a hill in the eastern section of the graveyard is an impressive Civil War memorial. The obelisk reaches toward the sky and is flanked by cannon. The cemetery is open from dawn to dusk.

3

HINGHAM

"HISTORY AND PRIDE"

Visiting Hingham is similar to time traveling. The town has been so well preserved, much of it untouched by suburban development and urban renewal that has plagued many other historic communities, that tangible pieces of the past are everywhere you turn. It is as if the visitor is stepping into a postcard from long ago. The length of Route 228, from Queen Anne's Corner into the heart of town and along downtown streets such as North, South and Central Streets, is lined with immaculately maintained original homes. In older towns such as Plymouth, a large portion of residences and businesses fell to the wrecking ball. Other agrarian communities such as Pembroke and Hanover have experienced larger sprawl as the former farms were turned into mini-malls and suburban tracts of housing. Hingham boasts roughly two hundred impeccably preserved antique homes. Hingham's history of European settlement, similar to that of Plymouth, was due to a group of religious dissenters, although this time they were Puritans. When Eleanor Roosevelt visited, she proclaimed it as the "most beautiful town in America." Since many Hingham families remained in town, with homes being passed down from one generation to the next, strict building laws were instituted to dissuade development. The town never faced a period of steep decline due to the ebb and flow of industry, so its historic character has been preserved into the twenty-first century. Unlike other antiquated towns, be it Deerfield, Massachusetts, or Wethersfield, Connecticut, Hingham's homes are fully occupied and are not museums with period furnishings.

The Old Ship Church is thought to be the oldest church in continuous use in the country. *Author's photo.*

The area settled as Hingham was part of the land of the Massachusett tribe and was eventually sold by Chief Wampatuck of the Massachusett in 1665, although the first European settlers arrived in 1633. It was initially known as Bare Cove for the shallow harbor, which at extreme low tide would present as practically devoid of water. The name was changed to Hingham in 1635 in tribute to the place of origin of the first colonists, Hingham, England. The group of settlers was led by Peter Hobart and Robert Peck. (Peck would eventually return to England a few years later.) Many of the early settlers of Hingham have descendants in town today. Names include Cushing, Loring, Thaxter and Hobart. Another famous Hingham last name is Lincoln. This Lincoln in question refers to the first ancestor of Abraham Lincoln to arrive in America. Reverend Hobart's clan numbered around forty-eight. The geography of Hingham was appealing since it was in proximity to Boston. Additionally, it had a natural harbor with an abundance of fish and shellfish in the tidal flats and woods full of trees to be used as lumber. In only a short distance, the topography ranged from oceanfront to woodlands with land soon cleared for pasture.

Hingham was best known for seafaring, although it has had some industry throughout its history, including woolen, saw and gristmills, an iron furnace, a ropewalk, a coal yard, a brass foundry and an umbrella factory. One of the industries that Hingham was best known for was the manufacture of woodenware and toys. The coopers and artisans made Hingham renowned for its crafts. Woodenware, wooden tools, containers and boxes handcrafted and beautifully designed put Hingham on the industrial map. Wood design was the forte of these craftspeople. Among the vessels for storage created in Hingham was the bucket, which gave rise to the nickname "Bucket Town." On the property of Peter Hersey, descendant of a longtime Hingham family, is the Reuben Hersey Toy and Box Shop, an old shed with a collection of artifacts from this period. (If you are interested in your own handmade Hersey bucket, visit www.herseybuckets.com.)

The original shipyard was located at the end of Ship Street. One of the primary catches in the waters of Hingham was mackerel. (In the twentieth century, Hingham would be a hotbed for manufacturing of a different kind—for the military. This is detailed in depth in the chapter titled, "Former Military Holdings.") Much of public land that attracts visitors for recreation has been utilized as military sites. These include Bare Cove Park, Wompatuck State Park, Turkey Hill, as well as the Hingham Shipyard, which is now a multiuse facility of restaurants, shopping and residences.

Another testament to Hingham's past within its present is the Cracker Barrel Store on Main Street. Today it is a popular mini-market, perfect for running in for essentials, a bottle of wine or a snack. For over two hundred years, it has been used for the same purpose, as a small store, originally selling dry goods and provisions. With Hingham being the home to the first descendant of Abraham Lincoln in America, a statue of the sixteenth president is seated in the middle of the town green. Queen Anne's Corner is the busy intersection near the Hingham/Rockland/Norwell town lines, where Routes 228 and 53 cross. Notorious Queen Anne refers to an eighteenth-century woman, Anne Whiton, who owned a tavern nearby. Although never married, she birthed six children out of wedlock. Some speculate that she was referred to as "quean" not "queen," with the term *quean* being a moniker of ill repute as that of a prostitute. In front of the Hingham Library on Leavitt Street is a wooden sign with the town name on it. This is reminiscent of a sign of like design that stands in the center of Hingham, England.

Today's Hingham borders Weymouth to the west, with the Weymouth Back River forming the boundary. Norwell and Rockland adjoin to the south, Cohasset is due east and Hull extends from the north as a peninsula jutting into the bay. The town of Cohasset was once within the boundary lines of Hingham. Accord Pond is the largest body of fresh water in town, and Hingham Harbor contains a few islands in the chain of Boston Harbor Islands. These include Sarah, Langlee, Ragged and Button Islands. Much of the land that was once purposed for military use has been refitted and left wild as conservation land devoid of development. On Main Street in the town center, the road's two yellow lines are replaced by a red, white and blue center strip. Hingham is an upscale bedroom town of Boston, although it has a vibrant downtown full of boutiques and eateries and is entirely self-sufficient. Spend an afternoon exploring, eating and shopping in downtown Hingham.

YOUR GUIDE TO HISTORY

Old Ship Church

107 Main Street, Hingham, MA 02043
781-749-1679, www.oldshipchurch.org

Built in 1681 on the site of the First Parish Church (1635) by the founder of Hingham, Reverend Peter Hobart, the Old Ship Church was constructed in the Gothic Elizabethan style, which was once prevalent in New England during the 1600s and 1700s. The Old Ship Church has the distinction of being the only church of its kind still standing. It was also used as the town meetinghouse. The "ship" moniker arises from the fact that the workers who constructed the church were shipbuilders. As a result, the ceiling is reminiscent of a body or hull of a boat turned upside down. This style, with its vaulted ceilings, recalls the medieval churches of England. The story goes that once the building was completed, the construction crew, which consisted of each male citizen of twenty years of age or more, consumed nineteen barrels of hard cider. This church has the reputation of being the oldest in Massachusetts and the oldest church in the country in continuous use. It has become the symbol of Hingham. Adjacent to the church is the Old Ship Church Burial Ground; the earliest gravestones date from 1672, before the construction of this church. This is the resting place of Hingham's earliest residents. This graveyard leads to Hingham Cemetery. Once Puritan, it is now a Unitarian Universalist Church.

Patriotism enhances Hingham's Main Street. *Author's photo*.

Hingham Cemetery

12 South Street, Hingham, MA 02043
781-749-1048, www.hinghamcemetery.org

The cemetery is of the garden style, patterned after Mt. Auburn Cemetery in Cambridge and Watertown, Massachusetts. It opened in 1838. Walk around the grounds to view various gravestone styles and keep a lookout for Maria Hooper's stone with a statue of the Angel of Grief huddled over the grave marker. This is a replica of William Wetmore Story's monument, which he designed for himself and his wife, located in the Protestant Cemetery in Rome. This statue, destined for Hingham, was constructed of Italian marble and shipped to the United States. Upon arrival in Boston, the crate was dropped and the statue smashed. Another copy had to be made. Bodies of the earliest settlers that were uncovered during the lowering of Main Street to allow the use of horse-drawn trolleys were interred in Hingham Cemetery and marked by the Settlers Monument. Also, the Tomb of the Three Ministers marks the remains of the first three reverends: Peter Hobart, John Norton and Ebenezer Gay. Upon exhumation, it could not be determined who was who, so the remains were placed under this tomb when transferred here. The area surrounding the Settlers Monument has original and replica headstones of some of the earliest residents. Another monument of note is a statue of an angel known as the Recording Angel, constructed by sculptor Larkin Meade. There is a bronze seal that commemorates the burial spots of Edward Farnsworth and Suzanne Clark. The proud statue of Governor John Andrew watches over the grounds. The Ames Chapel dates from 1887 and can be rented out for special events, even weddings! Please note, this burial ground is still in use.

Behind the Old Ship Church is an entrance to the Hingham Cemetery and the Memorial Bell Tower. *Author's photo.*

Madame Derby Academy "Old Derby Academy"

34 Main Street, Hingham, MA 02043
781-749-7721, www.hinghamhistorical.org

Founded in October 1784 as the Derby School, it is noted for being the first coeducational school in the country. Before this, all schools were gender specific. It was deemed an "academy" in 1797. The first preceptor, who was to teach all the academic classes, was Abner Lincoln. The school was the vision of Sarah Langley Hersey Derby, who was a widow twice over, both times of prominent men. She never had children but found a passion for working in education in her later years. She allotted the money to begin the school and to keep it running past her death. In 1852, boys and girls were allowed to cohabitate the same classroom. The 1818 Derby Academy building is located at 34 Main Street. It is operated by the Hingham Historical Society as a museum and visitor center. The building housed the academy until the 1960s, when it moved to its current location at 56 Burditt Avenue. The stately yellow three-story Old Derby Academy building is perched high above Main Street. It is also available as a rental space for functions.

The Old Ordinary

21 Lincoln Street, Hingham, MA 02043
781-749-7721, www.hinghamhistorical.org

This former tavern, which now houses a museum of Hingham history, was built in 1680. It was called an ordinary due to the fact that an "ordinary" meal was served here once a day at a predetermined rate. Its collections include paintings, furniture and artifacts related to the town. Among the paintings is that of a boat constructed at the shipyard in Hingham that was the first American vessel to reach China. The upstairs bedrooms are furnished, and its taproom has been re-created on the first floor. Among the memorabilia here is a pewter mug, used for imbibing libations by no other than Marshfield resident and famed statesman Daniel Webster. Across the street from the museum is the Benjamin Lincoln home (but the front of the house faces North Street), a descendant of Samuel Lincoln, an original Hingham settler. Lincoln was a general in the American Revolution under George Washington and is buried in the Hingham Cemetery.

Statue of Abraham Lincoln and the Samuel Lincoln House

Intersection of Lincoln and North Streets, Hingham, MA 02043

Located on the town green at the intersection of North and Lincoln Streets is a seated statue of President Abraham Lincoln, a direct descendant of early Hingham settler Samuel Lincoln. The pensive-looking president keeps watch over the green and has since 1939. Across the street from the green is both the Benjamin Lincoln home and that of Abraham's first descendant in the New World, Samuel Lincoln. The land in which the home is placed has housed Lincolns since 1649, with this structure built in 1721. The Samuel Lincoln home is at 170 North Street but is a private residence.

Historic Houses of Hingham

Drive or walk down many of its streets, and the historic houses that await you will not disappoint. Main, South, North, Central, Leavitt and East are among the roads worth strolling or driving along. The catch is these are viewable to be admired from the outside only, since most all are private homes. Take early settler to Hingham Matthew Cushing and look at a few properties acquired by members of his family. The home of Elisha Cushing sits at 692 Main Street and was built in 1714; this is a saltbox-style house. At 156 East Street is the home of Stephen Cushing, which was constructed in 1752. During a home project in the 1940s, a secret room was discovered near the chimney, and in the middle of the room was a pair of leg shackles. What is often referred to as the Cushing Homestead is a 1678 saltbox home that sits at 210 East Street. It was built for Peter Cushing by his father, Daniel. These are simply three examples of the fine residential architecture of this town.

World's End

Martins Lane, Hingham, MA 02043
781-740-7233, www.thetrustees.org, Admission $8 weekend/holidays, $6 weekdays

The most popular walking spot in town has to be World's End. Tucked away off of Martins Lane, World's End is a premier natural oasis, jutting out on a peninsula in Hingham Harbor. There is an admission fee. The terrain consists of sweeping meadows, salt marshes, tree-lined paths and a coastline with access to the water. Benches are scattered about to provide rest and reflection. Clear views of the Boston skyline are afforded to the visitors, but at this site, the city feels worlds away. It is worth a visit any time of the year. Fall leaves provide a lovely backdrop, cooling ocean breezes are plentiful in the summer and, in the winter, a cover of snow leaves the reservation stark, but serene. This was once an island at high tide, connected to the mainland, but it was dammed by farmers to access the land used for growing hay. In the 1880s, Boston businessman John Brewer had dreams of building an estate here. The famed landscape architect Frederick Law Olmsted was hired to design the grounds in 1890, but the building campaign never bloomed to fruition. The carriage roads of his vision still remain. World's End is actually considered part of the Boston Harbor Islands. The beauty and peace of this land were threatened by a housing development, but luckily it never happened. It was also proposed as both a site for the United Nations and later for the nuclear power plant that was eventually constructed in Plymouth.

4

SCITUATE

"SATUIT"

The town of Scituate's name is derived from the word *Satuit*, which means "cold brook" in the language of the Wampanoag. The Satuit Brook, which the town is named for, empties out into the harbor. Timothy Hatherly is known as the "Father of Scituate." He first arrived in the Plymouth Colony aboard the ship *Ann*. Early town records show English settlers arriving to this area in the mid- to late 1620s. The men who spearheaded settlement in Scituate were from Kent, England, and were collectively known as the "Men of Kent," a phrase often used when discussing the earliest arrivals to town. Scituate was officially incorporated as its own town in 1636. The first settlement developed around Kent Street on Third Cliff. The oldest building still standing in the town is the Barker Tavern restaurant. Originally built as the home of John Williams, it was historically known as the Williams-Barker House. During the years of King Philip's War, it was utilized as a place of refuge

Other than farming, much of Scituate's economy was based on the sea, including fishing, harvesting moss and shipbuilding. Shipbuilding on the North River was a hugely successful endeavor. The *Columbia*, which was the first American ship to sail around the globe, was built in 1773 at Hobart's Landing. Its name comes from the Columbia River, as the ship was also used to explore the Pacific Northwest. (Further details about this can be found in the Marshfield, Norwell, Hanover and Pembroke chapters.) Fishing is still a viable industry in town, although not as large as it once was.

A historic view of the Old Scituate Light. *Courtesy of the Scituate Historical Society.*

The current boundaries of the town were settled in 1849 after years of subtracting and adding land. Large changes in Scituate include Hanover breaking away to become its own municipality, and in 1849, South Scituate, eventually known as Norwell, became its own town. During the Portland Gale of 1898, the North River's course, which historically formed the town's southern boundary with Marshfield, was altered, which separated Humarock from the rest of the town. The only way to reach Humarock by land, which is still Scituate's possession, is through Marshfield. In the past, when speaking of their hometowns, townsfolk in Scituate often name-checked their village of origin rather than the whole town because village allegiance was strong. Today, many village names continue to be used: North Scituate, the West End, Minot, Mungo Corner, Humarock, Cedar Point, Sand Hills, Greenbush, Scituate Center, Scituate Harbor and Egypt. In 1846, the South Shore Railroad was built, eventually becoming part of the Old Colony Railroad in 1877. The railway connected Scituate to towns north and south of it and, on a larger scale, to major centers such as Boston. Passenger service was reinstated in 2007 on this line, with the MBTA's Greenbush commuter rail line terminus at the Scituate station of the same name.

Given Scituate's notoriously rocky coastline, the Massachusetts Humane Society helped save the stranded at sea. This morphed into the United States Life-Saving Service, which had two outposts in Scituate. Among the historic attractions in town are two lighthouses, the Stockbridge Grist Mill, the Old Oaken Bucket House and the Lawson Tower. Thomas W. Lawson, a businessman, designed an elaborate estate he named "Dreamworld"; the house no longer stands, but a tower on his property still exists. Rising near the center of Scituate is a gargantuan wooden structure that resembles a European castle's tower. Lawson designed this as a sheath for a water tower that the town wanted to be built. The castle-like structure is simply a casing for a mundane water tower. Built in 1902, it held water until 1988. It earned the status of an American/Canadian/Mexican Water Landmark, as it is of water-related historical significance.

World War II loomed large in town, not only with townsmen enlisting in the war effort but also with civilians back home. Rationing such items as food, supplies and electricity helped to conserve as part of the war effort. At the former site of the World War I Proving Grounds was the WURL Radio Station, which helped combat fascism overseas. Radio programs advocating the benefits of democracy were transmitted to four continents. They were heard in such lands as Norway, which was occupied by Nazi Germany, and France, both in free and Vichy France (German-occupied), rallying anti-fascist and pro-democratic sentiment. The station was founded by Walter A. Lemmon, a radio pioneer, who even attended the Conference of Versailles with President Woodrow Wilson as part of an appointed scientific group. Before and after the war, the radio station broadcast both cultural and educational programs. A blimp crashed in Pincin Hill from the Weymouth Naval Air Station on July 31, 1943. Luckily no one was killed, but tragically, seventeen servicemen from Scituate did lose their lives during World War II.

The South Shore and specifically Scituate found itself in the spotlight due to an event that happened one fateful night in March 1956. The 491-foot Italian freighter *Etrusco* was caught in a terrible blizzard off the coast of New England. The gigantic ship was en route to Boston from Germany when it ran ashore at Cedar Point. It landed parallel to the coast from the area of the seawall all the way down to the Old Scituate Light. The grounding was the last shipwreck of note that has occurred on the coast of New England. The Coast Guard had to wait until the next morning to rescue the Italian crew. For the next eight months, culminating in a relaunch of the ship on Thanksgiving Day 1956, the *Etrusco* lay grounded on the Scituate shore.

It became quite the tourist attraction, with visitors flocking to Scituate to view the freighter. Preceding its departure from Scituate, the *Etrusco* was christened with a new name, the *Scituate*. The fanfare caused by the wreck helped open the public's eyes to Scituate and was the impetus for people discovering the town and moving to the region. After the event, Scituate's population exploded.

Today, Scituate's economy is partially based on the sea, although recreational crafts are more present than working fishing boats these days. The farms that once dotted the landscape are mostly gone. Suburban development built the town up during the twentieth century, although Scituate is still a charming beachside community with a notoriously rocky coastline. Much of its history is tied to the sea; its present is too, albeit less for sustenance and more for fun. Both the harbor and North Scituate have retained their downtown atmosphere. Twenty-first-century Scituate is known for its harbor, numerous shops and restaurants, beaches and the two famous lighthouses in town. A nickname for the town is the "Irish Riviera," given its seaside location and its large population of Irish Americans. Sometimes the nickname references the whole South Shore.

Scituate is historically and presently tied to the sea. *Jaclyn Lamothe.*

YOUR GUIDE TO HISTORY

Much of the commercial district of Scituate is centered on the harbor. It is a fine place to stroll, shop and grab a bite to eat. To access the beach and other sites not in the harbor, a car is needed.

The Old Scituate Light and the American Army of Two

100 Lighthouse Road, Scituate, MA 02066
www.scituatehistoricalsociety.org/light

Every child in school learns of the heroes of the Revolutionary War, including George Washington, Paul Revere and even the antihero Benedict Arnold. The story of how the colonies won their independence from Britain has become common knowledge. Although the American Revolution has become ingrained in the story of our country, the next scuffle with Britain, the War of 1812, is often overlooked completely, even though it has been dubbed "America's second war for independence."

Given its coastal location, Massachusetts was a prime target for the British. Scituate, which is located south of Boston, provided easier access for the enemy due to its geographic location. Whereas Boston is naturally protected by the peninsulas of Hull and Nahant, Scituate is more easily reached. Two true heroes of the War of 1812 came from this small fishing village.

The Scituate Lighthouse is located at Cedar Point at the entrance to the town's harbor. It was built in 1811, and its first lighthouse keeper was a man named Simeon Bates. In June 1814, the town of Scituate was invaded by the British. Afterward, the townspeople decided that they needed a militia to protect them.

Simeon had many children, but on a fateful day during that same summer, two of his daughters, Rebecca, age twenty, and Abigail, age seventeen, were at the lighthouse by themselves. Rebecca was in the kitchen, and she noticed a frigate in the ocean. As she peered out from the top of the lighthouse, she could see longboats being filled with soldiers from the ship, rowing their boats toward Scituate Harbor.

At first, the girls thought of using muskets to fire at the redcoats but quickly reconsidered. Rebecca and Abigail saw a fife and drum. The fife had been in the family's possession, while the drum was left by the militia. They gathered the instruments, ducked behind a dune and played them as loudly as they could. One girl banged on the drum, while the other whistled into her fife the patriotic anthem "Yankee Doodle" as loudly as she could.

The confused British heard the drumbeat and fife melody and quickly turned around, for they thought the militia was assembled near the lighthouse. The British hoped that their presence would go unnoticed until it was too late for the Americans, but the two Bates girls foiled the British plans. The townsfolk marched over to the lighthouse, also thinking that the militia had assembled there, but instead found only two girls, two young women who saved Scituate Harbor.

In the lighthouse keeper's house is a painting from 1906 of the Bates girls, and a historic placard located on the lighthouse grounds relays the story of the two young ladies. Rebecca and Abigail lived to be old women and are buried in Union Cemetery. The Scituate Lighthouse was the eleventh lighthouse built in the United States and is one of the oldest lighthouses still standing in America today. With the emergence of Minot's Ledge Light located in the ocean off the shore of Scituate, the old lighthouse's prominence waned. The light went into a period of serious decline but was eventually purchased by the town. In the 1960s, the historical society was granted money to renovate and repair it, and in the 1980s, the lighthouse was added to the National Register of Historic Places.

Today, the lighthouse is owned by the Scituate Historical Society, and the current lighthouse keeper is Bob Gallagher, an active member of the historical society. Visit Bob's blog at oldscituatelight.blogspot.com for updates and news regarding the lighthouse.

Minot's Ledge Light

Located off the coast of Scituate

Whereas the Old Scituate Light is accessible by land and actually has a small public beach next to it, the town's other lighthouse, Minot Ledge Light, is located about a mile offshore in the Atlantic Ocean and close to the town's border with Cohasset. This lighthouse was built in 1850 but was tragically destroyed in 1851, only to be rebuilt stronger in 1860. The area where the Minot Ledge Light was erected was a spot ominous to sailors who were unfamiliar with it. This location had seen over forty shipwrecks between 1832 and 1841 alone, and it had led to the demise of many more sailors and boats prior to that. Unlike the Old Scituate Light, which has an attached house, the Minot Ledge Light keeper's house was onshore in Cohasset.

An unbelievable storm destroyed the ill-constructed original light in 1851. Although the keeper was ashore at the time, his two assistants, Joe Wilson and Joseph Antoine, were on-site. The gale decimated the lighthouse, with hardly a remnant of the building left, and took the lives of the two men. Although a new granite light was constructed in 1860 and has proudly graced the waters since then, the screams, cries and moans of the ill-fated lighthouse assistants have been heard reverberating from Minot Light. After the tragedy, lighthouse keepers tended not to hold their position for long. Bizarre events occurred, including the lens being inexplicably clean when the keeper checked it after a day of hard use. Another man woke to a whisper in his ear and saw a ghostly figure. One fisherman sailing by was attracted to the light by a howling man who started screaming in a nonsensical language when the fisherman got closer.

In contrast to the foreboding stories of the light, its nickname is the "I love you light," given the 1-4-3 pattern of its flashing tower. (The numbers relate to the letters in each word.) A replica of the top of Minot Light is located outside the Cohasset Sailing Club off Border Road. The light was even used for target practice; it was bombarded by airplanes unloading bags of flour instead of bombs.

Both Scituate lighthouses have stories to tell, one of heroism and one of catastrophe. While the nickname for Minot is the "I love you light," the Old Scituate Light is a popular place for engagements (it is where the author attempted to kneel on the rocky shore to propose), wedding photos and even beachside ceremonies. The grounds around Scituate Light are open to the public and include a beach, two jetties and a parking lot. Minot Light, located far offshore, is not accessible, but the replica can be viewed from the parking lot of the Cohasset Sailing Club at 19 Lighthouse Lane in Cohasset.

The Maritime and Irish Mossing Museum

301 The Driftway, Scituate, MA 02066
781-545-5565, www.scituatehistorical.org/maritime

A possession of the very active Scituate Historical Society, this museum is located in the home of Captain Benjamin James and dates from 1739.

The six exhibit rooms feature changing displays. Among the exhibits are information and artifacts from shipwrecks, since this town's coast was one of the most precarious in the nation. Also, there are rooms dedicated to lifesaving, newspaper headlines and boat models. Harvesting moss was a lucrative industry in Scituate. The red algae, nicknamed Irish Moss, was gathered and made into household products, including toothpaste, medicine and even beer. Tools used in the mossing process are on display at the museum. It is open every Sunday from 1:00 p.m. to 3:00 p.m.

Stockbridge Grist Mill

Country Way, Scituate, MA 02066
781-545-1083, www.scituatehistorical.org/mill

Speculated to be the oldest mill of its kind in the country, the Stockbridge Grist Mill was constructed by Isaac Stedman in 1640 after he dammed the First Herring Brook. The mill was erected along the pond that formed after the damming. Ten years later, John Stockbridge rebuilt the mill, and it appears much the same today. The Stockbridge and later the Clapp family were proprietors of the gristmill until 1922, when the latter family left it to the Scituate Historical Society, which is still the current owner. The mill gained a certain amount of fame when it was name-dropped by poet Samuel Woodworth in his poem "The Old Oaken Bucket." This is the mill he is referring to in his popular ode, reflecting fondly upon childhood. Although the entirety of the mill is not from the original period, much of it dates from the seventeenth century. It is located on Country Way, near the rotary where Routes 3A and 123 meet, on the eastern side of the road. The highlight of the poem is also in Scituate. Close by is the Old Oaken Bucket House, whose oldest section of the house dates from 1675, although much of the main section was built in 1826. The well and bucket referenced in the poem are still here and can be seen from the street. The house is located at 47 Old Oaken Bucket Road. Contact the Scituate Historical Society for more information.

Chief Justice Cushing Memorial State Park

Cushing Park Road, Scituate, MA 02066

This is one of the smallest state parks in Massachusetts. The memorial is dedicated to Chief Justice William Cushing. Cushing was a Scituate resident, born in 1732, and was appointed to the Supreme Court by none other than George Washington. Cushing was known for his stance against slavery. The small burial ground, accented by the relatively short Cushing obelisk, is a lesser-known attraction in town. The seven-acre park is located on Cushing Park Road, a side road off of Neal Gate Road, which connects Route 3A and Route 123.

5

DUXBURY

"INCORPORATED JUNE 17, 1637"

Traveling down Washington Street in Duxbury, visitors will be wowed by the number of preserved homes from Duxbury's era as a leader in shipbuilding from the late eighteenth to the mid-nineteenth century. Stately mansions line this road where former sea captains and captains of maritime industry once dwelled. Except for this small but prolific foray into wealth and mercantilism, Duxbury was once and became again a rural town whose main source of revenue was agriculture.

This region was known by the Wampanoag, who inhabited it for thousands of years, as Mattakeesett, or "place of many fish." Once the early Plymouth inhabitants were allowed to venture past village limits after seven years, established by their initial contracts with financiers, the northern tracts of land—the eventual towns of Kingston, Marshfield and Duxbury—were used for seasonal farming, eventually giving way to year-round residency. Duxbury was officially incorporated in 1637; the court granted permission for "Ducksborrow" to be a separate established town. The original land parcel included the towns of Bridgewater, which broke off in 1656, and Pembroke, which was the western part of town known for the abundant river herring found in the brooks and rivers. Pembroke became a separate town in 1712. Among the notable first residents of Duxbury was Myles Standish; the name *Duxbury* is most likely derived from a family estate in England, where Standish was born, Duxbury Hall. Standish lived along the coast of Duxbury known as the Nook—now commonly called

Powder Point Bridge leads to Duxbury Beach. *Author's photo.*

Standish Shores. Elder William Brewster, the religious leader of the Pilgrim separatists, took up residence in Duxbury. *Mayflower* passengers John and Priscilla (Mullins) Alden settled in Duxbury as well. Alden, a cooper, would become a senior member of the new colony's group, serving as an assistant to the governor, among other positions. Standish and Alden's precarious relationship is famously described by Henry Wadsworth Longfellow in his poem *The Courtship of Miles Standish*, in terms of the duo's competitive affection for Priscilla. Fittingly, the Aldens and Standish are buried a few cannon lengths away from one another in the oldest maintained cemetery in the country, better known as the Myles Standish Burial Ground. (Cannon length due to the cannons that adorn Standish's grave.) Many of Duxbury's place names are derived from its earliest settlers. Its streets alone include Alden Street, Priscilla Lane and Soule Avenue, named for George Soule, a passenger on the *Mayflower* who is also buried in the earliest cemetery. The path of early settlers from Plymouth up to Marshfield is known as the Pilgrim Trail. A loop from the path dating from 1637, known as the Ducksborrow Path, winds closer to the sea. Other spurs include the Bay Path, which heads west from Duxbury. Parts of this parallel today's Summer Street (Route 53) and Congress Street in Duxbury. Another spur starting in Duxbury was the Old Path to Pembroke. It also travels west but is located farther north than the Bay Path. Today's Mayflower Street and Congress Street (Route 14) follow this route.

During the years of the Revolutionary War, Duxbury was a proud patriotic town, as opposed to its neighbor to the north, Marshfield, which had a strong Loyalist sentiment. On Captain's Hill in South Duxbury, effigies of the British were burned in retaliation to the imposed Stamp Act. When regulars were quartered at the Thomas Estate in Marshfield (by request), a band of Patriots from Duxbury gathered together to confront them. The meeting did not happen—the arrival of British ships allowed the redcoats to flee. There were 270 men from Duxbury who enlisted to fight in the Revolutionary War. Men from Duxbury assisted the fortification of Dorchester, which helped end the British siege of Boston. In 1776, the fort at the Gurnet in Plymouth, located at the end of Duxbury Beach in Saquish, was manned by troops from Duxbury. Other Duxbury troops spent the terrible winter at Valley Forge and fought at Germantown, Pennsylvania, and Monmouth, New Jersey.

The most lucrative period of industry in Duxbury was its shipbuilding years. From the late 1700s to the mid-1800s, the town was a premier site for this industry. The part of town dedicated to this craft, as well as the homes of those who reaped the benefits of it the most, comprise a noted historic section today. Much of it is centered on Washington Street, but do not miss the loop toward the beach on Powder Point and King Caesar Roads. At the industry's height in 1840, there were around forty shipyards in town. The most profitable and well known of all the captains of industry of Duxbury was self-proclaimed King Caesar. His actual name was Ezra Weston, and he oversaw the rise of a shipbuilding company and firm. After he died, his son, Ezra Weston II, also adopted the moniker of King Caesar. The Weston fleet contained a large number of various ships, more than 110 of them. Additionally, the Westons operated a ropewalk (where rope is made) and a mill that employed many individuals. Weston I began the lucrative family business, and Weston II expanded it further. Under the latter, the largest boat ever built (at the time) was constructed. It was named *Hope* and weighed 880 tons. The materials used in the Weston boats were mostly locally sourced. The Weston home is an impressive Federal-style mansion on the aptly named King Caesar Road and is owned by the historical society.

Whereas many towns, take Plymouth for instance, keep reinventing themselves due to changes in fortune and industry, Duxbury began as a farming community, peaked with a shipbuilding boom but then settled back to its rural roots, only adding beach-loving out-of-towners to its repertoire upon the advent of the railroad in 1871. By the 1850s, the shipbuilding business in Duxbury had gone belly up, as high-powered steamboats and the railroad made the use for the older-model ships at Duxbury obsolete. The extension of the railroad from Boston, known as the Duxbury and Cohasset Railroad, shuttled in tourists who loved the expansive Duxbury seaside and beachfront as an escape from the congested Boston summers. An example of this boom was the creation of the Myles Standish Hotel, located near his former area of residency. Erected in this general area as a tribute to him in 1898, high atop a large pedestal is the monument to Myles Standish, with a standing Myles keeping watch over Duxbury Bay. (More about the statue in the "Forefathers" chapter.) Although the wharves are long gone, the stately homes of captains of industry and captains of the sea abound in Duxbury. The original grandiose architecture lines the streets. Travel Bay, Chestnut and especially Washington Streets, and these gems can be seen. Almost all of them are immaculately cared for. It is especially beautiful at Christmastime, when so many of these lovely homes, most of which are traditionally painted white with black shutters, are illuminated by candlelight in the windows. Duxbury, similar to many South Shore towns, has become a bedroom town of Boston, albeit a wealthy one, but has completed the amazing feat of retaining many of its original structures. In the twenty-first century, not only has Duxbury kept its old-timey, classic New England feel, but it has also been a hotbed of oyster cultivation. Duxbury is the home of Island Creek Oysters, a world-famous oyster farm whose distinct oysters have a rabid following. Additionally, other oyster farms and companies—such as Merry Oysters and Standish Shores—have sprouted up in Duxbury. Duxbury's most famous export was once its ships, but now it is the bivalves.

YOUR GUIDE TO HISTORY

King Caesar House

120 King Caesar Road, Duxbury, MA 02332
781-934-6106, duxburyhistory.org/private_tours, Admission $8–$10,
call ahead for private tour

In the National Register of Historic Places, the home of shipbuilding magnate Ezra Weston II, better known as "King Caesar," is a museum operated by the Duxbury Rural and Historical Society since 1967. The

The Myles Standish Monument on an autumn day. *Author's photo.*

Federal-style house, with its cheery yellow hue, white trim and black shutters, is especially appealing during the Christmas season. The home is available for tours. Traveling on King Caesar, Powder Point and Washington Streets, one experiences tangible evidence of Duxbury's lucrative shipbuilding past.

Art Complex Museum

189 Alden Street, Duxbury, MA 02332
781-934-6634, www.artcomplex.org, Admission free

A small but world-class museum is located on a back road in Duxbury on part of the original land parcel granted to John Alden. The Art Complex Museum houses the collection of Carl A. Weyerhaeuser, whose family amassed a fortune as one of the world's largest timber companies. Carl's father offered to buy him a Packard automobile when he graduated from Harvard. He declined the offer, instead opting for a Rembrandt. This insight into his life shows the Weyerhaeusers' dedication to the arts. Carl, at the persuasion of his wife, Edith, opened this museum to share his collection with the public. The family summered in Duxbury. The museum's modern architecture seems out of place in a town dominated by white and black Colonial homes, but at the same time, it merges nicely with its wooded setting. The museum is free and contains rotating galleries.

Sculpture on the grounds of the Art Complex Museum. *Author's photo.*

Upon entering, on the left-hand side is a special exhibit that changes frequently but also includes a Louis Comfort Tiffany stained glass. The permanent collection is displayed on a rotating basis and includes works by Rembrandt, Mary Cassatt and John Singer Sargent, as well as an extensive collection of Asian art (even a full-size Japanese tea hut) and many Shaker pieces. The fact that only a small portion is on display at a given time just gives more impetus to return frequently. The museum has intriguing modern sculpture throughout the grounds.

Sun Tavern

500 Congress Street, Duxbury, MA 02332
781-837-1027, www.suntavernrestaurant.com

The Sun Tavern in Duxbury has been one of its most popular restaurants since the 1930s. Dining by the blazing hearth is a perfect backdrop for a winter meal. The earliest part of the former home was built in 1741. It has a notorious history as the home of the "Duxbury Hermit," whose real name was Lysander Walker. Although Walker passed on in 1928, he is said to still walk the halls of the restaurant. Guests and staff have felt his presence. In one story, a candle relights itself after all had been blown out at the end of the night. In another, the police were called after an alarm was triggered—not by a human, but possibly by Lysander. The restaurant has been named the Sun Tavern since 1987. The menu is traditional American food with a mix of steak, seafood and pub grub. Speaking of a pub, the bar at Sun Tavern is quite inviting.

Powder Point Bridge

At the end of Powder Point Avenue, Duxbury, MA 02332

The original Powder Point Bridge, which connects Powder Point Road to Duxbury Beach, was built in the late nineteenth century, between 1892 and 1895. Due to its age, it was the longest and oldest wooden bridge in the world. Although the title of the longest wooden bridge still stands, the oldest is no longer, since the bridge was reconstructed during the 1980s after a fire in 1985 destroyed about seventy feet of it in the middle. The bridge spans the Back River near where it meets Duxbury Bay. The bay is bordered by Duxbury Beach and Saquish. The view from the bridge into the tidal flats or toward the bay is gorgeous. Additionally, the half-mile bridge itself is certainly photo worthy. If traveling by car, be prepared for a bumpy ride on the old wooden bridge.

6

OLD BRAINTREE

BRAINTREE AND QUINCY

Braintree and Quincy are both major municipalities on the South Shore. Quincy alone is Massachusetts's eighth-largest city. Today, Braintree is most closely affiliated with commercialism as the home of South Shore Plaza shopping mall. Historically, Braintree comprised the area of today's town, as well as the towns of Quincy, Randolph, Holbrook and a piece of Milton. Delineating what constitutes the South Shore is difficult. Some sources say it is only the towns directly on the sea; others include ones farther inland. Where does metropolitan Boston end and the South Shore begin? This question can be argued at length. For this collection, Quincy and Braintree are included as part of the South Shore, but Milton, Holbrook and Randolph are not.

The section of Braintree that is now Quincy was heavily populated. Historically speaking, it is hard to tell the story of Braintree without also chronicling that of Quincy and vice versa. What was once historic Braintree is often referred to as "Old Braintree." This chapter is separated into sections of Old Braintree, which includes the pre-European history of the area, as well as the town through the late 1700s. The Quincy section, or what was known as the North Precinct, continues with the town of Quincy as it separated from Braintree in 1792, with it earning city status in 1888. The last section is the history of modern-day Braintree, or the Middle Precinct. Of course, the history overlaps.

President John Adams's Peacefield, or the "Old House," now part of the Adams National Historical Park. *Author's photo.*

OLD BRAINTREE

The land that would become Braintree was important to the Massachusett tribe. Similar to Plymouth, when the English came to this region to settle, the Native American population had been severely decimated by disease. A historic site in the present-day town of Quincy is Moswetuset Hummock. This was the base of the Massachusett tribe sachem Chickatawbut. Sources say that Moswetuset is a variation of Massachusett, the name of the tribe and the future name for the commonwealth. The hummock, which is a small earthen mound, is located at the northern end of Wollaston Beach and at the base, or the southernmost part, of the Squantum Peninsula. Moswetuset has also been translated as "place of the big house" or "place of the great chief." In 1621, Myles Standish and Squanto landed here. The Monatiquot River, which flows through Braintree, was important for Native Americans as a source of transit and for fishing. The four-and-a-half-mile river has been documented as the site of twenty camps for local Indigenous peoples. The river's name translates to "place of many villages" as well as "lookout place," "abundance" and "at the deep tidal stream."

The first European settlement, albeit short-lived, began in 1625, headed by Captain Richard Wollaston. The original European name for this land was Mount Wollaston. A group of indentured servants led by Wollaston wintered here, but he left the region for Virginia and did not return, dying a year later. Wollaston and Thomas Morton sailed from England to join the Plymouth Colony in 1624. A disagreement arose between Wollaston's group and those in charge, who felt that they should not trade guns and liquor with the Native Americans. Wollaston's group left to begin anew, farther up the coast. Upon Wollaston's departure, Morton was in charge. Morton and Wollaston had a disagreement of their own. Morton started a trading post, and the settlement was known as Merry Mount. Merry they were, as lascivious behavior abounded. With the purpose of infusing local Indigenous customs into their own lifestyles, the settlers engaged in drinking and dancing around the maypole in 1627. The nearby Pilgrims did not look kindly upon their neighbors, who they felt were practicing pagan rituals and were rumored to be cavorting with local Native American women. Morton's settlement did not exist for long, as he was arrested by Myles Standish and sent packing back to England due to his dirty deeds after banishment to the Isle of Shoals off the coast of Portsmouth, New Hampshire. There is a monument to Morton's maypole on Sunset Hill off Samoset Avenue in the Merrymount neighborhood.

In 1634, Mount Wollaston became part of Boston, and land grants were even offered for people to settle here. This region was far from the center of Boston, which looked very different from today. The original Shawmut Peninsula, where Boston was settled, was only connected to the mainland by a thin isthmus. Much of what is thought of as Boston proper is actually made from landfill. This rural region's first official landowner was Reverend John Wilson. He was granted 365 acres in the southern section of today's Quincy, from Squantum to the Weymouth Fore River. Three other early landowners with substantial land claims were William Coddington, Atherton Hough and Edmund Quincy. Another early landowner, Edward Tyng, settled in what is now Randolph. Mount Wollaston consisted of the land that is Quincy today, except for North Quincy, which was part of Dorchester. As development ensued, rumblings started in 1637 for this region to establish its own town independent of Boston.

In May 1640, the town of Braintree was officially established, since it was granted its own church, which was the fifteenth in the Massachusetts Bay Colony. The church was built in 1639. Today's current parish's church was built in 1828, nicknamed the Church of the Presidents. It is the final resting place of Presidents John Adams and his son John Quincy Adams, as well as their wives, First Ladies Abigail Adams and Louisa Catherine Adams. It was built by noted architect Alexander Parris, constructed of granite culled from nearby quarries. The origin of the name *Braintree* is debated. Sources point to various origins, none of which, thankfully, are due to a literal description of what is found in the town. (There are no brains growing on trees.) Many speculate that the town is named for Braintree in England, but no early settlers had direct ties to the town. This was often the case when choosing a name. One thought is that representatives of the Braintree Company, from the County of Essex in England (where Braintree is located), came to this area, led by the future founder of Hartford and thus Connecticut, Thomas Hooker, and crossed the Neponset River to settle but were then ordered to migrate farther north for habitation, eventually choosing what became Cambridge. Another version of its origin is that the town is a derivative from the Old Saxon word Branchetreu which translates as "town near the stream." Given that the Monatiquot River bisects Braintree and was historically an important freshwater source, this has validity.

The first settlements of Braintree were located in what today is Quincy. It was not until 1708 that the church was split into precincts, with the Middle Precinct, also called Monotocut, being the area currently known as Braintree. Today's Quincy was known as the North Precinct. In 1665, Josiah Wompatuck, sachem and son of Chickatawbut, officially sold the lands that became Braintree, as well as other municipalities in the commonwealth, to England. The first meetinghouse was located near Cliveden Street. The first cemetery is now known as Hancock Cemetery and is located at the center of Quincy. In 1731, the third parish of Braintree was established in what is now Randolph.

Old Braintree was primarily a farming community. Dairy farms and orchards dotted the landscape. Firewood was exported to Boston. The Monatiquot River was the lifeblood of the middle section of town. It was a source of livelihood for many in Braintree and eventually became an important industrial site. In the northern section of Old Braintree, fishing, trading and shipbuilding thrived. Ships were made in Germantown, which was the first preplanned industrial development in the country.

The ship *Massachusetts*, built in Germantown in 1789, was the largest American-made boat up to that time. The Germantown neighborhood was established in 1750. Given the area's coastal nature, fishing was a large industry, and even whaling took place here. Germantown was noted for its glassmaking. One industry that Quincy is synonymous with is granite quarrying. King's Chapel in Boston was constructed of the local rock. This brought more widespread awareness to the local stone, which put a (temporary) cease on using it for out-of-town projects. Similar to many towns in this region of the South Shore, shoe making was a steady industry. It started as a small cottage industry, growing into a major economic force. As royal governor of Massachusetts Bay Colony, John Winthrop's son, also named John Winthrop, established an iron furnace in Braintree. The Winthrop Iron Furnace, the first commercial ironworks in the country, began in 1845. It was situated on the banks of what is now known as Furnace Brook in West Quincy. The furnace ceased operation soon after and would eventually be morphed into the highly successful ironworks in Saugus. Winthrop would go on to found the city of New London, Connecticut, and become a royal governor of the Connecticut Colony. Iron manufacturing did migrate south to present-day Braintree after the closure of Winthrop's operation.

One cannot speak about the history of Old Braintree and not dedicate space to its most famous residents: John, Abigail and John Quincy Adams and John Hancock. The Adams family is forever linked with the town. John Adams was born in Braintree on a farm. His father was a deacon of the Congregational Church. Adams was schooled at Harvard and became a lawyer, most notably defending the British troops in court after the Boston Massacre. In Braintree, Adams wrote a document known as the Braintree Instructions that outlined a rejection of the Crown-imposed Stamp Act. Adams's fame as a founding father, his work as part of the Continental Congress, role as commissioner to France, time as an ambassador in Europe and years as first vice president and then president of the United States are well known. Adams and his wife, Abigail, bought his final mansion, known as Peacefield, in 1787, moving in a year later. Due to his time abroad and time in national office, including that of the presidency, it was not until 1801 that he was finally able to live there continuously. In 1779, Adams penned the Constitution of Massachusetts, which became the basis for the U.S. Constitution. His son John Quincy was born close to the family homestead. He purchased both his father's house and this home later in life and lived in Peacefield. John Quincy Adams was the sixth president of the United

States. These homes are all part of the Adams National Historical Park. The First Parish Church is located nearby and is the final resting place of the Adams presidents and first ladies. John Hancock, the first governor of Massachusetts, signer of the Declaration of Independence and president of the Continental Congress, was also born in Braintree, although he is most closely associated with Boston.

QUINCY

"City of Presidents"

Motto: "Manet—It Remains"

Quincy was officially established as a separate town in 1792 and named for Colonel Josiah Quincy. This encompassed the North Precinct of Braintree as well as a part of Dorchester, now referred to as North Quincy. Quincy continued to grow, with major industries such as shipbuilding, quarrying and fishing. Given the depths of Quincy's waters, shipbuilders who were once on the North River relocated to Quincy to accommodate further shipbuilding needs. The Bunker Hill Monument was erected in the early to mid-nineteenth century as a tribute to the Revolutionary War battle, and the monument surpassed King's Chapel as the most famous Boston landmark made of Quincy granite. Its success was twofold. It was the first obelisk-style monument in America (soon to be overshadowed by the Washington Monument), and it also drew major attention to the granite being quarried at Quincy. It was designed by Solomon Willard, who moved to Quincy in 1825 in preparation for the construction of the monument and remained a resident until his death in 1861. He is buried in Hall Place Cemetery, which is next to St. Mary's Church.

A canal was built in 1826, but even more impressive was the railway being constructed concurrently with the canal. Along with the success of the granite quarry came the first commercial railway in America. It was known as the Granite Railway and connected West Quincy, the site of the quarries, and Neponset. There were fifty-four quarries in all, primarily located in West Quincy. Along with the quarries were stonecutters and quarrymen who were employed there, as well as blacksmiths who manufactured the tools used to cut the stone. Quarry work brought waves of immigrants to the Quincy shores. Many ethnic groups, including Swedes, Scots, Irish and

Germans, flocked to Quincy to work at the quarries. Eventually, a wave of Finnish immigrants arrived. St. Mary's Church, built in 1845, became the first Catholic church and primarily served the immigrant population.

In addition to granite quarrying, the other industry that Quincy is associated with is shipbuilding. The property that was once the site of George Thomas's shipyard became the Fore River Shipyard, initially begun by Thomas A. Watson. The history of the Fore River Shipyard is detailed in depth in the chapter about the South Shore's military history.

The Old Colony Railroad was established in 1845. This drastically changed the character of the town, as neighborhoods sprouted along train routes instead of near water sources or other natural centerpieces. Quincy was officially granted city status in 1888 and today is one of the commonwealth's largest. With a population of 94,616 in 2017, Quincy was the eighth-largest city in the state. Its proximity to Boston has always been in its favor. It has a unique distinction of being a suburb and an urban center in its own right. Many commuters to Boston call Quincy home, but similarly, other workers commute to Quincy for employment. Among its largest employers is the supermarket chain Stop and Shop, which is headquartered here, as is Arbella Insurance. Harvard Pilgrim Health Care has a large office in Quincy. It is also where two major American brands began, Dunkin' (Donuts) and Howard Johnson. In addition to the famous Adamses, other famous Quincy residents include the actor John Cheever and the surf guitarist Dick Dale. Its neighborhoods are varied and distinct. Quincy runs the gamut from the downtown, full of high-rise office buildings, to Houghs Neck, with its beachside feel. Wollaston Beach is one of the metropolitan area's most popular summer destinations.

The city is chock-full of history and is even known as the "City of Presidents," but to the casual visitor, these sites can be easily missed. At times, mid-twentieth-century architecture obscures the historical nature of the city. It is similar to the town that once encompassed it, Braintree, whose history and identity have been shaped in the twenty-first century by the fact that it sits at the crossroads of two major highways, Route 93 to Boston or south to Route 95, as well as Route 3, which takes travelers to Cape Cod. In modern times, Braintree is more synonymous with one of the largest shopping malls in New England, the South Shore Plaza, and the highway interchange, colloquially known as the notorious "Braintree Split."

BRAINTREE

Incorporated 1640

Much of the earliest of Braintree's history has been included in the preceding section about Old Braintree, and ironically, much of what was considered Braintree is now Quincy. Just like navigating the treacherous Braintree Split highway interchange, these towns' histories are confusing at best. Another confusing aspect of Braintree is that although it is known as the Town of Braintree, it officially entered cityhood in 2008, at least according to the State of Massachusetts's guidelines. This section focuses on the former Middle Precinct of Braintree and, after 1792, what was a separate municipality from Quincy. Although this book does not include Randolph and Holbrook, both were part of Old Braintree as well.

Three rivers wind through the town; Moore's Farm and the Cochato combine to form the Monatiquot. Along this river was the key to much of Braintree's industry. Winthrop's iron furnace, upon leaving Furnace Brook, moved to the banks of the Monatiquot and stayed there until 1653. The

The tower at Thayer Academy proudly looms large in Braintree. *Author's photo.*

plentiful bog iron in the area drew the founders to this locale. A larger ironworks was established by John Hubbard in 1682. A large-scale operation, the whole area it encompassed was known as the "Iron Works District." Its location is near the present-day Mill Lane. As in Weymouth, Plymouth and Scituate, river herring was important to the lives of Indigenous people and English settlers. The ironworks dam blocked the passage of fish. In 1736, when the ironworks was operated by Thomas Vinton, the Town of Braintree paid him £300 to stop production and let the fish swim. Great Pond, which is the terminus of the Monatiquot and its tributaries, was the historic endpoint for the herring run. Herring was used more as fertilizer than food for human consumption. This same year, 1736, there was a vote in favor of ridding all blockage of the fish on the river. By 1817, dam owners were mandated to allow passage for the fish by law in Braintree.

Clearly, the river herring have been an integral part of Braintree's history. Even with the protection and the regulations on dams, industry also played an important role in Braintree. On the Monatiquot, even though only four and a half miles in length, there were nine mills on its banks. Initially, milling was localized, with a gristmill and a sawmill powered by the river. Similar to the subsistence farming that provided enough food to live on, the milling that happened here was to grind corn or flour for consumption. One site, at the corner of Washington and Plain Streets, has been a place of industry since 1643. Throughout the years, it has been the location of many plants, among them Blake and Revere Copper Foundry, Monatiquot Rubber Works and Armstrong Cork, the latter finally shuttering in 1996. This location is the current Massachusetts Registry of Motor Vehicles and the Bayshore Athletic Club at the site of the former Armstrong plant. Other factories in town included various textile mills, tack factories, a chocolate factory, shoe factories and paper production. Among the paper made here was manila. Manila, the sturdy hard stock paper, was processed from ropes made of hemp originally from the Philippines. The largest of the shoe factories was Slater and Morrill Shoe Company. This was the infamous site of a robbery that left the paymaster and his guard dead. In this case, it was not the killing of two innocent workers that grabbed headlines; it was the trial and execution of the supposed murderers. The world is familiar with the names of Sacco and Vanzetti to this day. The murder and robbery occurred at the South Braintree factory on April 15, 1920. There was not substantial evidence that the two men perpetrated the killings, but they were found guilty and set to face execution nonetheless. A general consensus was that their treatment was due to the fact that they were anarchists and Italian immigrants. Protests and outrage reverberated locally and worldwide, but the two men were put to death via electric chair on August 23, 1927.

There were eleven shoe factories in Braintree between the 1830s and the 1950s. The Slater and Morrill Company was on the land currently occupied by the Pearl Plaza Shopping Center on Pearl Street. Braintree's own electric company was founded in 1892 and is currently still municipally owned, which is a rarity in the twenty-first century.

After World War II's population boom, Braintree was forever changed, coupled with the advent of Route 3 and the ease of obtaining an automobile. Braintree in the mid- to late twentieth century was redefined by commercial interest. As manufacturing on its rivers ceased, the waterways were obscured by concrete. Braintree's shopping district, in the form of the mall and strip malls, is a popular destination. Similar to Quincy, its history is not in clear view, but unlike Quincy, its historic features are not as well publicized. Recently, though, there has been a movement to bring Braintree's natural areas back to focus. Money has been set aside to allow access points to the river for recreational activities such as kayaking and canoeing, with greenspace accompanying some of the riverbanks. Work is being done to demolish dams to provide further access for animal and man. Braintree's downtown and East Braintree are thriving with businesses and restaurants. Thayer Academy, which has been open since 1877, continues to serve as a premier private high school on the South Shore. And of course, the shopping plazas keep buzzing with activity.

YOUR GUIDE TO HISTORY

Adams National Historical Park

1250 Hancock Street, Quincy, MA 02169
617-770-1175, www.nps.gov/adam/index.htm, Admission $15

The Adams National Historical Park is a collection of buildings that were once in the possession of John Adams and his family. This park is unique in that the whole tour experience is available only via trolley. Visitors can drive or walk by the homes separately, but tours and access to the grounds are available only as part of the whole package. The historic site consists of three homes (John Adams's birthplace, John Quincy Adams's birthplace and Peacefield, the later home of the Adams family) and the Stone Library.

Moswetuset Hummock, the seat of Sachem Chickatawbut of the Massachusett tribe. *Author's photo*.

The tour starts at the modern visitor's center located at 1250 Hancock Street. Free parking is available (with validation) at the Presidents Place Parking Garage on Saville Street. It is walkable from the Quincy Center MBTA (Red Line) stop.

The first two homes were purchased by Deacon John Adams, John Adams's father. Incredibly enough, the homes that are part of the park stayed in the Adams family until 1893. When not occupied by family, they were rented out to tenants. From 1893 to 1940, the homes were bequeathed by the family to Quincy and operated by the historical society. In 1979, arrangements were made between Quincy and the national government to take control of the property as a National Historical Park. This is the premier site on the South Shore for Revolutionary War–era history. Just a note, these properties are located in the midst of busy commercial city streets, not isolated on large tracts of land. The birthplace of Abigail Adams, famous in her own right, is in nearby Weymouth.

John Adams Birthplace

133 Franklin Street, Quincy, MA 02169

The birthplace of John Adams was originally built by Joseph Penninman in 1681. It was acquired by Adams's father in 1720. John Adams was born here on October 30, 1735. It is in the classic saltbox architectural style. At its height, the farm that the house was part of consisted of 188 acres. Corn was the primary crop grown, and livestock were kept on this farm. It is located at 133 Franklin Street in Quincy. Deacon Adams left the home to John's brother Peter Boylston Adams. John later bought it from Peter.

John Quincy Adams Birthplace

141 Franklin Street, Quincy, MA 02169

Also built in the saltbox style, this home, purchased by Adams's father in 1744, was known as Penn's Hill. This home was built by Samuel Belcher in 1663. Upon John's marriage to Abigail Smith, the Adamses settled in this home. John Quincy Adams, John Adams's oldest son, was born here on

July 11, 1767. While the family lived here, John's birthplace was rented out. Adams's office in this home was where the Constitution of Massachusetts was penned. Later in life, John Quincy and wife, Louisa, came back to this home to summer during the years of 1806 and 1808.

Old House at Peacefield and the Stone Library

135 Adams Street, Quincy, MA 02169

Colloquially known as the "summer White House," this was home to John and Abigail later in their lives. This home is also referred to as the "Old House." John Adams and family moved into the home in 1788 but did not live here for any substantial amount of time until his years as an ambassador in Europe, vice president and president came to a close. In 1801, he returned to settle for good. This home was built in 1731 and was occupied by the Adams family between the years 1788 and 1927. It was the home of John and Abigail Adams, John Quincy and Louisa and further generations of Adamses, many of whom became prominent in their own right. The property's interior includes period furnishings and artifacts. There is a beautiful garden on the property as well.

In 1873, the Stone Library was built next to the property. This is a collection of around twelve thousand books that were in possession of the Adams family and was the worksite of descendants Charles Francis and Henry Adams as they penned historical volumes. The whole National Historical Park is open seasonally from late April to early November.

Church of the Presidents

1306 Hancock Street, Quincy, MA 02169
617-773-1290, www.ufpc.org, Donations welcome

Nicknamed the Church of the Presidents, the United First Parish Church is the final resting place of John and Abigail Adams and John Quincy and Louisa Catherine Adams. The congregation dates to 1636, with the first church erected in 1639. This is the fourth church as part of this congregation in Old Braintree or Quincy. It was constructed with financial help from a bequest from John Adams. It was constructed of Quincy granite by Alexander Parris, whose other accomplishments include Pilgrim Hall Museum in Plymouth and Quincy Market in Boston. The church is available for tours, including the presidential crypt. The crypt also has information regarding the first families. Tours are available seasonally, in sync with those at the Adams National Historical Park.

Josiah Quincy House

20 Muirhead Road, Quincy, MA 02170
617-994-5930, www.historicnewengland.org/property/quincy-house, Admission $5

Colonel Josiah Quincy spawned a lineage of highly distinguished descendants, including others bearing his exact namesake. Among them were three who became mayors of Boston, some who held various political titles and one who became president of Harvard University. The City of Quincy is named for this first Josiah, who started it all. Quincy Market in Boston is named for his grandson Josiah III, the Harvard president and politician. This house, which is now operated as a museum owned by Historic New England, offers a look inside, featuring fine examples of Revolutionary War–era furnishings. Known as Lower Farm, this home once had a serene landscape with views stretching into the bay. It is open for tours on the first and third Saturdays of the month from June 1 to October 15. It is located in the Wollaston section of Quincy.

Wollaston Beach

Accessed via Quincy Shore Drive, Quincy, MA 02170, Admission free

This picturesque beachfront over two miles in length is an urban oasis, accessible by the MBTA (Wollaston stop on the Red Line) and drivable via Quincy Shore Drive. At the northern end is Moswetuset Hummock, the seat of the Massachusett tribe. It is the largest beach in Boston Harbor. The waters of Quincy Bay are highlighted by skyline views of Boston beyond and that of the Harbor Islands.

Thayer House

786 Washington Street, Braintree, MA 02184
sites.google.com/site/thebraintreehistoricalsociety/the-thayer-house

The home of General Sylvanus Thayer is a historic property that is now under the jurisdiction of the Braintree Historical Society. He lived at the home during his childhood, from his birth in 1785 to 1793. This circa 1720 house, constructed by Nathaniel Thayer, has been expanded and altered, with its current status dating from 1800. Sylvanus Thayer's nickname is the "Father of West Point." On the side of the home is a cannon that was given to the town by West Point. The building is a fine example of the ever-popular saltbox style, and the home and period furnishings were given to the historical society in the 1950s. There are exhibits in the museum of military and railroad history, as well as an assemblage of women's handheld fans that were manufactured in Braintree. It is operated as a museum, although as of this writing, there are no regularly scheduled hours. Diagonally across Washington Street is Thayer Academy, and just to the south is Thayer Library. The Thayers were most certainly an important Braintree family.

7

MARSHFIELD

"HOME OF DANIEL WEBSTER"

Of any town on the South Shore, Marshfield's name is the most apropos. Although the land area of Marshfield is 28.62 square miles, traveling from one end of town to the other is a feat. As the crow flies, the miles are few, but hypotenuse roads are scarce. This is due to the rivers and marshland which comprise much of the town. Through most of its history, Marshfield has been agrarian in nature; however, the town is dominated by the water. In addition to the Atlantic Ocean, which forms its eastern border, the North, South and Green Harbor Rivers helped shaped Marshfield's economy. Marshfield's fourth river is the Cut River. In addition to farming, Marshfield's other main industries were shipbuilding and fishing, the latter of which is still thriving today. In the twenty-first century, the town has become a booming bedroom community of Boston, with a population a little under twenty-six thousand. Due to Marshfield's rural beginnings, it lacks many of the features of communities with larger town centers such as Hingham, Plymouth and Quincy. By no means does it lack history though. From its ties to famed statesman Daniel Webster to its role as a Loyalist stronghold during the years of the American Revolution, Marshfield's past is storied and intriguing. Boston cannot take the only credit for outward rebellion against the tea tax; this small town was the site of another tea purging ceremony. Marshfield was officially incorporated in 1640, although it was settled by Edward Winslow, a *Mayflower* passenger, in 1632.

The visage of Daniel Webster greets visitors to Marshfield on Route 3A. *Author's photo.*

Along with much of the lower South Shore, the land that would eventually be known as Marshfield, then known as Missaucatucket, was home to the Wampanoag tribe. With the arrival of the Separatists, commonly known as the Pilgrims, to Plymouth, this land was included in the original Plymouth Colony. Similar to Plymouth, the land was sparsely populated by Native Americans due to a widespread epidemic. Many artifacts have been found in Marshfield that have led scholars to believe that it was once a prime hunting location.

Winslow is among the names to know in Marshfield, as the town was founded by Edward Winslow, with his succeeding generations among the most prominent residents in town. Winslow was born in Droitwich, England, and joined the Pilgrims when they lived in Leyden in the Netherlands. Much is named for him and his family in Marshfield today. Winslow married Susanna White after her husband died during the first brutal winter of 1621. Winslow had been married previously to Elizabeth Barker, who died in March 1621. White had two children, Peregrine and Resolved. Peregrine was the first Pilgrim baby to be born in the colony, as he was birthed on the *Mayflower* as it was docked in what is now the harbor of Provincetown. (The first child born to the Pilgrims was Oceanus Hopkins, who was born at sea.) The first marriage in Plymouth Colony was between White and Winslow. Winslow negotiated peace with the Wampanoag and had a lasting relationship with Grand Sachem Massasoit. Winslow even visited the sachem when he was on his deathbed. Winslow himself was governor of the colony three times and introduced cattle from England to the Plymouth Colony. He was the ambassador to England from Plymouth. Winslow and White had five children of their own, including Josiah, who would be the first native-born governor of the Plymouth colony.

Josiah did not offer the same kind of benevolence toward Native Americans as his father did. For instance, Josiah sold off their land even when it was against the law to do so. When his actions were found illegal, he changed the law to suit his needs. Wamsutta (or Alexander) took over as grand sachem once Massasoit died. His life ended allegedly due to sickness, but the circumstances were mysterious. His brother King Philip (or Metacomet) felt that Josiah Winslow had something to do with Alexander's demise. This was one of the main causes of King Philip's War, which began in 1675. In southern New England, the conflict ended in 1676, but it spread to northern New England, where it concluded in 1678. Josiah Winslow had been commander of the colony's army since 1659 and was governor during the outbreak of the war. Winslow led the British soldiers at the Great Swamp Fight in current-day South Kingstown, Rhode Island. A vicious battle ensued, with the main Narragansett village burned and the killing of not only men but women and children as well. Prior to the English's campaign, the Narragansett were neutral; this battle caused irreversible damage to the tribe. Although Josiah Winslow was less tolerant of Native Americans, he was more lenient toward Quakers. He was governor from 1673 to 1680. The Winslow House, built in 1699 by Josiah Winslow's son Isaac, is known as Careswell and is located on the family estate. Today, it is a museum.

In addition to Missaucatucket, Marshfield has been called "Green's Harbor," for early resident William Green. It was also called Rexham and even Oxford, as it was dubbed by Captain John Smith as he explored the New England coast in 1614. The Town of Marshfield today comprises many distinct villages: Brant Rock, North Marshfield, Marshfield Hills, Marshfield Center, Green Harbor, Center Marshfield, Seaview, Rexhame, Ocean Bluff and Fieldston. Ocean Bluff's former name was Abington, and Marshfield Hills used to be called East Marshfield. The change occurred due to mail being sent to East Mansfield instead. Agriculture and fishing played a major role in the sustainability of early Marshfield. The North River fish species included river herring, shad and trout. The first church was established in 1640 and the first gristmill erected in the 1650s. One of the oldest sites in Marshfield is the Pilgrim Trail, also called Green's Harbor Path (named for William Green), which early settlers utilized to travel from and to Plymouth. This was originally a Native American path. Parts of it can still be accessed today, although some of it is on private property. The driveway of the Daniel Webster Estate and cemetery is on this route, as is part of the Pilgrim Trail road, which is across from the Webster lot. It crosses Ocean Street (Route 139) near Bourne Park Avenue. It was the first commissioned road in the Plymouth Colony. The path travels from Plymouth through North Plymouth, into Kingston, Duxbury and through Marshfield, ending in Humarock. The training green was in the center of town.

Eventually, the Plymouth Colony and the Massachusetts Bay Colony were joined together under the province of Massachusetts in 1691. As the eighteenth century progressed, wealthy Marshfield families such as the Winslows and the Thomases continued to prosper. The Thomas family, similar to the Winslows, were early settlers in Marshfield. In 1645, William Thomas obtained 1,500 acres of land to establish the estate that would be in his family until its acquisition by Daniel Webster in 1832.

Unlike many towns whose Patriot sentiments were widespread, Marshfield was a stronghold for Loyalists. In 1774, townspeople signed the Tory Resolutions, which declared that they would stay true subjects of the king. Earlier, when protests shook the streets of Boston against the Stamp Act, there was an outcry in Marshfield against the opposition. As tensions grew in the colonies and the Revolutionary War was on the horizon, the conflicting sides were antagonistic. On June 19, 1776, at a town meeting in Marshfield, citizens called out King George as a tyrant and declared their own declaration of independence. With stark opposing sentiments toward the revolution, trouble was brewing. The written words, sent to Nehemiah Thomas, who was Marshfield's representative in the General Court, accused the king of killing Americans and ruining property. Like Boston, Marshfield witnessed the quartering of British troops, although this was at the request of Tories who were lodged at Nathaniel Ray Thomas's estate. The Associated Loyalists of Marshfield numbered around three hundred, and their central meetinghouse was the Winslow House. These families of gentry class enjoyed their position in society under the Crown. After the Revolution, the former Tory stronghold of Marshfield did not allow the Loyalists to easily assimilate back into the community. Thomas's estate was taken, and he fled to Halifax, Nova Scotia. Some Tories were sent off to prison in Plymouth, while others were put under house arrest, forbidden to leave their property except to attend weekly church services. Other Tories were banished, and some were forced to pledge their loyalty to the Patriot cause. Of course, not all residents of the town were Tories. Conversely, patriotism also ran strongly in Marshfield, as exemplified by the Tea Rock burning, which is explained later in the chapter.

Due to Marshfield's geography, shipbuilding became a major industry and one of the first of its kind in New England. Not only were a number of boats built at the shipyards, but some were of historic significance as well. Large schooners, which were constructed at shipyards on the rivers, were led out to sea at the confluence of the rivers and the ocean, where the current Rexhame Beach is. On the North River (not just in Marshfield), one thousand ships were built from the 1630s to the 1870s. Packet boats transporting mail and cargo were used to sail between the North River and Boston. People would greet the boats at their time of arrival with the intent to purchase their contents. In Nelson Memorial Forest, there is a historic packet landing which is visitable. Other shipyards included that of the Rogers family, which was near Little's Bridge (the area where Route 3A spans the North River between Marshfield and Scituate today), and they also had a shipyard at Gravelly Beach at the end of Cornhill Lane. Brooks and Tilden's shipyard was located near Union Street Bridge. White's Ferry was a major ship manufacturer on the North River, near Humarock, which began operation in 1705. There was also the William Taylor yard. At the future site of Little's Bridge was a ferry that dated from 1637. A ferry ran on the North River at today's Union Street Bridge before 1700, originally run by Elisha Bisbee. Later, a toll bridge was built at this site in 1801; in 1850, it became free. Ferries were important in Marshfield, providing direct service over waterways. The North River shipyards are discussed further in the Norwell, Scituate, Hanover and Pembroke chapters.

Marshfield's schools have always been a point of pride. The first schoolhouse was built in the 1640s and remained there until 1857. Known as the South School, it was one of the oldest in the region. In 1789, the town was separated into school districts, with a school board overseeing them in 1826. The Clift Rodgers Free Library was established in Marshfield Hills in 1897. Today it still operates as an independent library, unrelated to the town library, the Ventress Memorial Library. Speaking of Ventress, Seth Ventress's name is on both the school administration building and the library. Ventress was a highly successful mason in Boston who was from Marshfield. Upon his death, he left $10,000 to the town to erect a municipal building that would include room for a library. The building came to hold not only the library, but also a high school and the town hall—it even contained a vault and two holding cells for prisoners in its basement. Today, it is the school district administrative offices and is located at 76 South River Street.

The railroad through Marshfield was on the spur of the Duxbury/ Cohasset branch of the Old Colony Railroad. Throughout its history, Marshfield remained a rural town. In 1900, there were 1,810 citizens. As in other agrarian towns, the younger generation did not stay in Marshfield; they often traveled to cities such as Boston to find work. In 1876, the town's streets were named, and those names still stand today. In addition to shipbuilding, there were a small number of shoe factories in Marshfield. Although industry was sparse, there was an ironworks at Furnace Brook, as well as nail factories and cotton mills powered by the South River. Additionally, the brooks that feed into the North River powered mills, including at least four on the Two Mile Brook. Hay was harvested for the livestock, and strawberries were also cultivated.

Although Daniel Webster was born in Salisbury, New Hampshire, he is synonymous with Marshfield. He was raised in a farming family and attended college at Dartmouth. Daniel Webster is most known for his years as a lawyer, orator and statesman in New Hampshire, Massachusetts and Washington, D.C. He was a member of Congress and secretary of state under the presidencies of William Henry Harrison, John Tyler and Millard Fillmore. He was known as the "Defender of the United States Constitution" and brokered the 1842 Webster-Ashburton Treaty, which delineated boundaries between Maine and New Brunswick and quelled tensions between the United States and Great Britain. He strongly believed the Union must stay together in the face of adversity. Webster first discovered Marshfield while returning from a fishing trip in Sandwich on Cape Cod. Sandwich was a favorite vacation destination of the Websters. In Marshfield, he was a guest of Captain John Thomas on his way back to Boston. He fell in love with the town and the land; thus Webster purchased the Thomas estate in 1832. John Thomas was the son of Nathaniel Ray Thomas and descendant of town forefather William Thomas. Daniel Webster lived on the estate until he died in 1852, although he split his time between Massachusetts and Washington, D.C. Eventually, his lot totaled roughly 1,800 acres, encompassing even the Winslow House. Farming was a passion of his. Among the animals he raised were cattle, sheep, poultry, peacocks and llamas. He was known as the "Farmer of Marshfield." He brought an awareness to agriculture that eventually helped establish markets on the town green by the South Marshfield Farmer's Club in 1862. These agricultural meetings were the early inspiration for the Marshfield Fair. The fair has existed since 1867, with the incorporation of the Marshfield Agricultural and Horticultural Society.

Webster's estate, known as Green Harbor, included a dairy cottage, a farmhouse, a fisherman's house and his office. Although his home burned in 1878, it was rebuilt two years later. This is the Queen Anne–style Victorian mansion that stands on the property today. The house contains paraphernalia that has symbolism to Webster's life. The Daniel Webster Wildlife Sanctuary Audubon Society is on land that belonged to him. (It is accessible at the end of Winslow Cemetery Road.) The Webster Estate currently sits on only fourteen acres, but much of the surrounding neighborhood is on land that once belonged to him. The Webster Estate is now used as a museum and function facility. Additionally, a part of the former estate, Webster's Wilderness, is conservation land.

The oldest cemetery in town is the Winslow Burying Ground, accessed via Winslow Cemetery Road and located toward the end of the street, on the left-hand side. Here lies the resting place of such notables as Susanna White Winslow, Peregrine White and Josiah Winslow. (Edward Winslow's commemorative plaque in the cemetery does not mark his burial place, for he died in the Caribbean while on a naval mission for England against the Spanish and was buried at sea.) Famed opera singer Adelaide Phillips is also interred here, as are members of the prominent Thomas family. Adelaide Phillips was born in Britain in 1833 and lived until 1882. She was known far and wide for her beautiful singing voice. Phillips moved to Marshfield in 1860 and lived in a mansion on Webster Street. This home burned in 1990.

Daniel Webster's tomb and the family plot are adjacent to the rest of the burial ground and surrounded by a cast-iron fence. Two of Webster's sons were killed in battle: Major Edward Webster died in the Mexican-American War, and Colonel Fletcher Webster perished at the Second Battle of Bull Run of the Civil War. Both of them are buried in the family plot. The present site of the cemetery was the location of the first meetinghouse, which was built in 1641. It was sold in 1657 and replaced by a church close to the present one in the center of Marshfield. There is a settlers' memorial honoring the early men and women who called Marshfield home, and in Marshfield Hills, there is a Civil War memorial to the soldiers from town who were killed in the war.

The present path of Route 139 between Green Harbor and Brant Rock travels over the Green Harbor Dike. It looks innocuous enough, but it was the site of one of the biggest issues of contention to plague Marshfield. So strong were sentiments that disgruntled townsman Henry Tolman attempted to blow up the dike using dynamite in the 1890s. The dike was built in 1872 to prevent the saltwater from inundating the land. Farmers had called for a dike for years because the salt water was detrimental to their crops, but the fishermen were against the dike. They thought that the dike would cause sandbars to form, which would mean they could only access the ocean and return to the harbor at higher tides. Even today, the harbor is dredged in regular intervals to ensure passage to the sea. The sentiment among fishermen was strong, as they felt that this ruined the harbor they needed for their livelihood. In 1898, the dike was to be removed by legislation, but the governor used his veto power and struck it down.

The Portland Gale of November 27, 1898, would forever change the geography of Marshfield. Out-of-towners often inquire as to why Humarock is part of Scituate but is only accessible through Marshfield and does not connect to any other piece of land in Scituate. Today's North River meets the sea between the Third and Fourth Cliffs. This is due to a tidal wave that broke through the land at this point and created a new outlet for the river. It is here where the North and South Rivers converge. Because of the storm, roughly 400 lives were lost and over 150 ships wrecked. Four Marshfield residents died. The causeway between Scituate and Marshfield was decimated, as was the train bridge over the river. In the early 1840s, government assistance was requested in cutting a hole in the beach between the Third and Fourth Cliffs. Representative John Quincy Adams came to visit the location. The government deemed this not feasible due to the damage it would cause the islands and nearby meadows. Not wanting to hear no, some townspeople took matters into their own hands, employing shovels, picks and axes to create their own cut through. Soon after its completion, Mother Nature had her way and filled it back in.

Named for the brant geese that frequented the beach, Brant Rock was the center of activity and recreation in Marshfield. Vacationers enjoyed the beachside activities, staying at hotels such as the Churchill, the Brant Rock House and the Fairview House (Inn). Brant Rock was a popular tourist destination for those escaping the heat of the urban environment of Boston. The railroad provided transportation for tourists or seasonal residents visiting Marshfield. Two communication firsts occurred in Brant Rock. Inventor Reginald Fessenden constructed an antenna at Green Harbor Point. The 420-foot tower was destroyed in 1917, but the base of it still exists and bears a plaque. It is located in the RV park at the end of Ocean Street and can also be accessed via Central Street. In January 1906, Fessenden was able to transmit a Morse code signal across the Atlantic Ocean to another tower that he operated in Machrihanish, Scotland, and received a message back. It was the first two-way transatlantic communication of this kind. Later that year, on December 24, 1906, Fessenden broadcast the first radio transmission to ships on the Eastern Seaboard. Instead of the typical Morse code, the transmission consisted of a speech by Fessenden followed by the song "O Holy Night" played on the violin. In the twentieth century, the neighborhood included a movie theater and was the site of ever-popular bonfires on the beach.

If the Portland Gale shaped Marshfield geographically, the Brant Rock fire of 1941 changed the town architecturally. The blaze began on an exceptionally windy day, April 21, 1941, during a spring season that lacked precipitation and ripped through the neighborhoods of Ocean Bluff and Fieldston. Gone were 446 homes out of a total of roughly 600 structures altogether, all engulfed in flames that day. Among the other buildings lost were the casino, three hotels, a church and the post office. Driving on Ocean Street, Route 139, from the center of Marshfield, a marked architectural difference is noted, differentiating buildings from before and after the fire. In the past, homes were packed together, much closer than they are today. This was one factor that led to the massive amount of destruction caused by the inferno. Also significant was the fact that the fire department was composed strictly of volunteers.

Similar to much of the South Shore, with the advent of the construction of Route 3, Marshfield's population boomed. The once small agrarian community blossomed into a bedroom town of Boston, with much of the architecture on Plain Street and Ocean Street (Route 139) utilitarian commercial buildings that hide clues to the town's past.

YOUR GUIDE TO HISTORY

Tea Rock and Marshfield's Tea Party

The commemorative plaque is located off of Moraine Street, across from Tea Rock Gardens, Marshfield, MA 02050

Boston was not the only site for tea desecration in retaliation for the tax put on tea by the Crown. In Marshfield, Deacon Nehemiah Thomas led the

A view of the South River from Marshfield's rail trail. *Author's photo.*

confiscation of tea in hopes it would deter trouble. The taking of the tea was not enough for some. On December 19, 1773, a group of Patriots, led by Benjamin White and Jeremiah Lowe, raided the home of Thomas to obtain the tea. (Other sources say it was the Old Ordinary, on the corner of Ocean and Moraine Streets, which is still there and now houses businesses.) Nearby homes that still had large quantities of tea were also raided. No matter the exact location of the tea confiscation, the large amassment of tea was hauled to what was from then on known as "Tea Rock," where it was set ablaze by Jeremiah Lowe and destroyed. As retribution, a tax was levied on those from town who did not denounce the tea burning. Tea Rock Gardens and Tea Rock Lane are among the names in modern Marshfield to allude to this historic event. Tea Rock was in this general area but was destroyed due to construction. A plaque in the woods commemorating the event is off Moraine Street on the eastern side of the road across from Tea Rock Gardens.

The Fairview Inn

133 Ocean Street, Marshfield, MA 02050

In addition to hosting celebrities, including Babe Ruth and Boston mayor James Michael Curley, the inn illegally smuggled in liquor during Prohibition by using the tunnel that connected the building to the ocean below. (Historically, Marshfield was a dry town until the twentieth century.) This hotel, built by Martin Swift in 1874, burned to the ground in 1998 but was rebuilt on the same site.

Brant Rock Tower

21 South Street, Marshfield, MA 02050

When traveling to the beachside community of Brant Rock, expect seaside cottages, a seawall and numerous restaurants—oh and a seventy-foot, eight-story concrete tower rising above the village. Literally towering above Brant Rock and located in the middle of the commercial area is the Brant Rock fire-control tower. It was built during World War II as part of the system of defense of Boston Harbor. Once the tower at Saquish was demolished, this was the southern point of defense for the greater Boston region via the water. From this tower, watchful eyes can view 180 degrees on the lookout for enemy ships or U-boats. It became a single-family home, with rooms on each floor, making it the tallest single-family house in the state. The Holly Hill neighborhood on the Marshfield side of Humarock once was the site of a fire-control radar. The Brant Rock Tower is located on Ocean Street in Brant Rock. It is the only tall concrete structure jutting high above the rest of the community. The tower has only one window on each side on floors two through five; the top three levels have a panoramic view.

Double Eagle I Balloon Flight

In September 1977, a ballooning record was set for the longest recorded balloon flight. Maxine Anderson and Ben Abruzzo launched from Marshfield in an attempt to cross the Atlantic Ocean in their hot-air balloon, the *Double Eagle I*. Unfortunately, their crossing was not a success,

Damon's Point in Marshfield looking toward Scituate. *Author's photo.*

as they had to abort their mission off the coast of Iceland. After leaving from Marshfield, they came close to colliding with Mount Katahdin in Maine, and the balloon was thrown off course due to a violent storm in Canada. It propelled them in the direction of Greenland. A year later, the team was successful, breaking their record of the Marshfield flight. This time, they departed from Presque Isle, Maine, and landed in France on a balloon named the *Double Eagle II*. Off of Grove Street is a small road called Double Eagle Drive in commemoration of this flight.

South Shore Railroad in Marshfield

*Access points in various locations throughout town
including on Ocean Street and South River Street*

The Duxbury and Cohasset Railroad was incorporated in 1867 and completed in 1871. It was known as the South Shore Railroad. From Duxbury, it joined with the Old Colony line in Kingston. In Marshfield, the train had five stops. They were East Marshfield/Marshfield Hills, Sea

View, Centre Marshfield, Marshfield and Webster Place/Green Harbor. It cost the Town of Marshfield $75,000 to build the railroad. Because of the train line, vacationers from the city and factory towns frequented the beaches and spurred a boom in cottage building, resulting in an increasing influx of summer visitors. The railroad was sold to the Old Colony Railroad for $15,000 by Duxbury, Scituate and Marshfield, with each town receiving $5,000. This left the town with a debt of $70,000. The Old Colony Railroad was purchased by the New York, New Haven and Hartford Railroad in 1893. The last train rumbled through Marshfield in 1939. Parts of the former train line are now walking paths for the public.

Marshfield Historical Society properties

65 Webster Street, Marshfield, MA 02050
781-834-0100, www.marshfieldhistoricalsociety.org

The Marcia Thomas House, located at 65 Webster Street, is the current home of the Marshfield Historical Society. The Cape Cod–style home dates from 1835 and is brown with maroon trim. It is open on every first Sunday of the month from 1:00 p.m. to 4:00 p.m. Thomas, whom many consider Marshfield's first historian, was the author of the book *Memorials of Marshfield*. The museum contains around 3,500 Marshfield-related artifacts that have been collected since the founding of the Historical Society in 1913. The extensive collection includes portraits, maps, letters and furniture. Marcia Thomas was born in Marshfield in August 1800, and upon her death, she donated money to construct the Settlers Memorial, which was placed in the Winslow Cemetery. In 1997, the home was moved to its present site and became the headquarters of the society. Also owned by the historical society and located close to the Marcia Thomas House at the corner of Webster and Careswell Streets is the Winslow School. This schoolhouse was built in 1857 and used until 1910, as it was one of the eight schools in town. It was built on land that was given by the family of Daniel Webster. The historical society acquired the white schoolhouse in 1925. During the 1920s and '30s, the former society president, Edward Ford, ran the Careswell Shop, an antique store, on site. The school was opened to the public in 1968 and became the headquarters of the historical society in 1969. It remained the site of the society until it was replaced by the Thomas House. Tours are available upon request.

Daniel Webster Estate

238 Webster Street, Marshfield, MA 02050
781-834-0548, www.thedanielwebsterestate.org, Admission: Donations accepted

The original home plot of 1,000 acres was awarded to Marshfield forefather William Thomas in 1640. The home remained in the Thomas family until it was sold to Daniel Webster in 1832. Tory Nathaniel Ray Thomas requested the presence of British troops on his land in 1775. Thomas fled to Halifax, Nova Scotia, during the persecution of the Tories. The Thomas estate was seized by Massachusetts but turned back over to the Thomas family in 1791, to Captain John Thomas, who was an advocate of the revolutionary cause. Daniel Webster was a guest of Thomas on his return to Boston from fishing vacations in Sandwich. It was here that Webster fell in love with the property and Marshfield. After Webster acquired the property, he took pride in farming the land. His estate expanded to 1,800 acres, including the Isaac Winslow House and the property that is now Mass Audubon's Daniel Webster Wildlife Sanctuary. The estate was known as Green Harbor and is pictured on the seal of Marshfield. On his property were other buildings, including his law office and agricultural structures such as barns and a dairy cottage.

The estate built by Nathaniel Ray Thomas burned in 1878, but two years later, Caroline White Webster, Daniel's daughter-in-law, commissioned Boston architect William Gibbons to erect the current estate. After the Webster tenure, the property changed hands and the land was subdivided for years, creating the home plots for many of the houses in the neighborhood. During the middle of the twentieth century, it was the site of Camp Daniel Webster, a camp for children. It was purchased by Marshfield in 1996. The home, which now sits on a much-reduced fourteen acres, is a museum operated by the Daniel Webster Preservation Trust. In addition to being a museum, it is used for functions such as weddings and private parties. There is an annual summer family fun day, tea ceremonies are held in the warmer months and during December, the home is bedecked in Victorian Christmas décor of yore. The large Queen Anne–style home is a sight to see around the holidays. The rooms are full of Christmas trees, mannequins styled in nineteenth-century garb and festive green and red galore. The home also includes elements of Webster's life embedded in the architecture. This includes Webster's coat of arms and a large portrait of him over a fireplace. The home is highlighted by a large porch, a grand staircase (perfect for that magical entrance, especially at weddings), chandeliers and ponds on the grounds. In 1882, President Chester A. Arthur visited the estate for the centennial of Webster's birth. Since then, it has welcomed many other dignitaries. His law office is also on site after having been moved back to the property in 2015. For many years, it sat preserved on the site of the Winslow House. The driveway of the estate is on the route of the Pilgrim Trail. Throughout the history of Marshfield, this property has been witness to the ever-changing world. From the site of a trail used by Native Americans and early settlers and home of a town forefather to the estate of Marshfield's most famous resident and today's preservation of it, the property has witnessed over four centuries of history.

8

HULL

"NANTASCOT"

When the geography of the town, as in Hull's case, is a thin peninsula protruding into the sea, the way of life, economy and population are heavily dependent on the water. The shape of Hull is reminiscent of an L turned upside down. The length of the town, along with its accompanying harbor island, Peddocks Island, provides a natural boundary to Hingham Harbor. In the summer months, Hull's population booms, with many tourists and residents enjoying nature's beauty and the entertainment found in the town. Hull is bordered only by Hingham and Cohasset, as there is no other land access from any direction except the south. Being as isolated as it is, it is the farthest to reach from most towns on the South Shore. It takes about half an hour from the tip of Hull to the nearest highway (Exit 14 off Route 3).

Approaching Hull from Route 228 in Hingham, the initial neighborhoods soon give way to the Nantasket Beach area. This was once the bustling seaside amusement village of Paragon Park. Traces of its past still remain, including Paragon Park Carousel, the original merry-go-round that was part of the park. Other remnants such as the arcade and summertime T-shirt shops also recall an earlier time. The main attraction here is the beach. Nantasket, a long beach full of fine sand, is one of the most popular seaside locales south of Boston. (It also attracts many city dwellers given its proximity to Boston.) This section is also teeming with restaurants, bars and the recently renovated Nantasket Beach Resort. This has been referred to as either the Jersey Shore or the Coney Island of the South Shore (especially in the days when Paragon

The storefronts of Nantasket Beach are closed for the season. *Author's photo.*

Park was at its height). The next stretch of the peninsula is largely made up of neighborhoods, with its main street, Nantasket Avenue, lined with restaurants and shops, mostly for the local, not the tourist. As Nantasket Avenue bends left, the neighborhoods are filled with stately Victorian homes. Visiting the tip of Hull is worth the wait. This area contains the Hull Lifesaving Museum and Fort Revere, which sits high atop Telegraph Hill (both described in detail in the chapter "Former Military Holdings"). Hull's public library and high school are also both here. There are amazing views, including that of the Boston Light, Boston's iconic lighthouse, which is situated on Little Brewster Island. This light dates from 1783 and is the second oldest in the country. It was the location of an earlier beacon erected in 1716, the first built in the future United States. At the tip of the peninsula, the views of Boston are gorgeous. A sunset over Hull Gut (the strait that separates the mainland from Peddocks Island) is unmatched and should be witnessed at least once. Pink and orange hues that melt over the Boston skyline are truly breathtaking.

Hull's history, similar to its present, is reliant on the sea. From its early days with its Native American inhabitants and its use as a trading post of the Plymouth Colony to its heyday as an amusement park destination and its ties to the Coast Guard, Hull's history is unique and water-bound. The land that would become Hull was known as Nantascot, or "place between the tides," by the local Native peoples. Other variations of the name's origin are recorded as "at low tide" or "the strait." It was utilized as a trading post by the Pilgrims as early as 1621 and maintained by Myles Standish. The town was settled a year later, in 1622, but officially incorporated in 1644. Its name is derived from the English town of Kingston upon Hull. Farmland claimed much of the end of the peninsula of Hull during its early years, as farming and fishing were major ways of life. Hull's history has strong ties to the sea. Other industries that have been important for the town include trading and lifesaving (since the notoriously rocky coast has been the site of many a shipwreck). Its location, forming a natural boundary sticking into the sea, has tied Hull's history to military defense, including protection of Boston Harbor. In 1776, Fort Independence was built on Hull's Telegraph Hill, which became the eventual site of Fort Revere in 1901. Fort Duvall was located on nearby Hog Island, now known as Spinnaker Island, with a man-made isthmus connecting it to the mainland. Traces of the fort can be seen underneath the condominium complex. (Later, this was used as part of a Nike missile site along with the present-day Webb Memorial State Park located across the bay in Weymouth.) Peddocks Island, at the tip of the Hull peninsula, was the site of Fort Andrews, a turn-of-the-twentieth-century fort built to protect Boston Harbor from the south. Fort Andrews was one of the largest fort complexes in the Boston Harbor defense system. The military facility once contained around thirty buildings. Peddocks Island also contains a series of World War II–era fire-control towers. There is another of these towers on the mainland of Hull on Point Allerton. Peddocks Island is accessible by ferry, and it is part of the Boston Harbor Islands chain. Camping is available on site.

The Massachusetts Humane Society, the precursor to the Coast Guard, had lifeboats and huts on Hull. Later, as the home of the Coast Guard, Hull would remain a prominent lifesaving location. The Hull Lifesaving Museum details the history of this aspect of the town. The first hotel arrived for tourists when the Sportsman Hotel was built in 1825. In 1840, steamboats arrived from Boston. The early twentieth century brought a new throng of visitors to Hull, as Paragon Park, the iconic amusement park near Nantasket Beach, opened its doors. It shuttered in 1984, with the carousel being the final remaining ride from that earlier era. Paragon contained the thrilling roller coaster Giant Coaster, an extensive boardwalk, waterslides and an arcade with pinball machines. Some of the old beachside honky-tonk feel remains, but high-rise condominiums have been built on the site of much of the park. On warm summer days, Nantasket Beach brings in a large number of visitors, but it pales in comparison to when Paragon Park was in its prime.

YOUR GUIDE TO HISTORY

Paragon Park Carousel and Museum

205 Nantasket Avenue, Hull, MA 02045
781-925-0472, www.paragoncarousel.com/home, Museum suggested donation, $2

Paragon Park closed its doors in 1984, and a subsequent auction rid the Nantasket shoreline of most of the theme park nostalgia. The carousel remains as a reminder of the past and is just as popular today as it was when it opened in 1928. The carousel's design is four rows of beautifully painted, hand-carved horses. The famed Philadelphia Toboggan Company manufactured much of it. (There is speculation that it also contains elements of design by the Dentzel Carousel Company of Philadelphia, which the Toboggan Company acquired in the late 1920s when it went out of business.) The Philadelphia Toboggan Company specialized in roller coaster design, but the merry-go-round is a true work of art.

A group of investors saved the park from relocation and vowed to keep it in Hull. It was moved not far from its original site, next to the Victorian-era train station. This building is noted for its clock tower and currently houses a museum detailing the history of Nantasket and the park. The museum's era of focus concludes with the closing of the park. The entrance to Paragon Park was a grand affair, beautifully constructed with archways highlighting the entranceway. While today's setup is not quite done on this grand scale, the Nantasket area of Hull still has enough entertainment to provide an afternoon of fun. Along with the carousel and museum (and of course the beach), there is ice cream located in the former train station, a miniature golf course and an arcade. Recently, a group of individuals purchased much of the Nantasket strip with hopes of returning it to some of its old glory. The carousel, open seasonally from Easter to the last week of October, is located at 1 Wharf Avenue in Hull. The museum is open on Tuesdays to Sundays from 1:00 p.m. to 5:00 p.m. The carousel was added to the National Register of Historic Places in 1999. While in Hull, make sure to take a spin to the past; the carousel is a perfect mix of nostalgia and pure fun in the present.

The promenade of Nantasket Beach. *Author's photo.*

Hull Gut

Located at the end of Main Street, Hull, MA 02045

Hull Gut is the deep-water channel that is located at the end of Pemberton Point, the tip of the Hull peninsula. It is a prime fishing spot—instead of accessing the deep water via watercraft, one has the ability to stand on land and cast into depths of the sea typically farther offshore. Fourteen-year-old Rosie Pltenhof made history when she swam back and forth from Peddocks Island to Pemberton Point in Hull. It took her only twenty-two minutes round trip. Today, swimming is prohibited due to the swift current of the channel, along with the steep drop-off from coastline to the deep ocean. The name "gut" may sound funny, but all it means is that it is a natural channel through deep water. I'm not much of a fisherman myself, but I do recommend watching the sun dip below the horizon over Hull Gut, as it is one of the prettiest sunset spots on the South Shore. The parking lot, often full of sunset-seekers, attests to its popularity. Follow Main Street to the end of Pemberton Point, historically known as Windmill Point (and also the site of a wind turbine) to locate the parking lot.

9

PLYMPTON, HANSON, HALIFAX AND CARVER

AN AGRICULTURAL ADVENTURE IN THE SOUTH SHORE

The towns that comprise the South Shore are debated. Sometimes, the South Shore is strictly those towns that border the coast; other definitions include towns as far inland as Hanson and Halifax. Commonalities among the coastal towns are industries that sprang up due to access to the ocean and activities associated with the sea. The agrarian towns of Plympton, Hanson, Carver and Halifax feel as if they are in another state in comparison to their seafaring neighbors. Farming, animal husbandry and village life are still prevalent in these communities. Although housing subdivisions and mini malls can be found, much of the rural character remains. These towns include unique farms that are open to the public, such as Sauchuck and Just Right Farm in Plympton, Nessralla Farm in Halifax and the Blueberry Farm in Hanson. Plympton and Halifax are among the best towns on the South Shore to witness fall foliage. In comparison to other more wooded areas of Massachusetts, the coastal region's autumn display is not as vibrant. Carver is associated with its cranberry crop. These towns, with their shady groves of trees, horse pastures and winding roads, lend nicely to the season when the air becomes crisp, apples ripen and witches abound.

Cemetery gates in Plympton. *Author's photo.*

PLYMPTON

"Incorporated June 4, 1707"

Plympton retains much of its rural nature from bygone years. Before the arrival of Europeans, the land was inhabited by the Wampanoag. The first English settled here in the mid-1600s. This land became the parish of West Plymouth in 1695. In 1707, Plympton was officially incorporated and its first meetinghouse built, but the town was much larger than it is today. Plympton was named for Plympton, England. The current borders were delineated in 1862. Originally, the towns of Halifax and Carver were part of Plympton, as was land that now belongs to Kingston and Middleborough. Although the Industrial Revolution brought factories and mills manufacturing shoes, shovels, cotton and lumber to Plympton, industrialization did not have a large impact on the town. The center of town is incredibly quaint. Its historic town center sits along Main Street (Route 58), with the graveyard forming the northern boundary and Mayflower Street to the south. This neighborhood was added to the National Register of Historic Places for

Plympton's tercentennial celebration in 2007. The town green was used for militia training and at one time was the location of a town pound, where stray animals were placed when they escaped from farms. The farmers would have to pay a fine to claim their lost animals. Also on site were stocks and an armory. The homes that line Main Street and nearby Mayflower are fine examples of architecture between the years of 1706 and 1894, including Georgian, Federal, Greek Revival, Queen Anne and Colonial Revival styles. Two cemeteries are in this district: Hillcrest and the burial ground behind the Plympton Congregational Church. Hillcrest, located at the northern end of the parcel of land, dates from 1706 and includes phenomenal examples of stone carving. The Soule family of stone carvers and Nathaniel Fuller were tombstone artisans who are prominently featured. The death's head, a reminder in colonial society of what is to follow this life, is etched on many stones. Those of the Soule carvers include what is referred to as a "Medusa" death's head—the wild cropping of hair resembles Medusa's serpentine locks—with a heart-shaped mouth. As years progressed and the view of death was less up front, the death's head was replaced by cherubs and eventually supplanted by the urn, which commemorates the individual's life instead of heeding a warning to the onlooker. Eventually, the term *cemetery* would usurp burial ground or graveyard. The word is derived from the Greek term for resting place, certainly, a more friendly way to look at death than the brutal *burial ground* or *graveyard*, which tells it exactly as it is. Rural towns farther away from urban centers, in this case, Boston, were later in making the switch in gravestone design, due to the styles of the carvers and the slow pace at which trends traveled outside of the city. Also in the Plympton Historic Center is the library, which dates from 1905, and the school, now town offices, from 1935. Other sites include a shoe shop, a grange and a general store. The first meetinghouse was built in the mid-1690s. Two other meetinghouses were erected before the First Congregational Church was built in 1830. A burial ground, established in 1850, is located behind it. On the green is a Civil War monument, which is a statue of a soldier; a memorial to other wars; and a plaque embedded on a boulder, placed by the Daughters of the American Revolution, dedicated to the most famous resident, Deborah Sampson. Another historic district is in North Plympton at Harub's Corner, which is at the corner of Lake Street and County Road.

Deborah Sampson is Plympton's most lauded citizen. She was born in the town in 1760 and is best known for her war effort in the American Revolution. Women typically played a peripheral role during the war and were not actual combatants. Sampson was unusually tall (five feet nine inches) for a woman of the period and was sturdily built. She disguised herself as a man and enlisted in the army as Robert Shirtliffe in Uxbridge, Massachusetts. She fought and was wounded by musket balls in the leg during a battle near Tarrytown, New York. Sampson refused a doctor's aid since it would reveal her true identity. A year later, in 1783, she was sent to Philadelphia, where she became sick and needed medical help. Here her gender was revealed, but she was honorably discharged at West Point and has become a true legend and a feminist role model. Sampson was a descendant of governor of the Plymouth Colony William Bradford.

HANSON

"Incorporated 1820"

Although Hanson was not incorporated until 1820, the history of the region goes back much further. The land was inhabited by Indigenous peoples for thousands of years prior to the arrival of Englishmen. This area was between two settlements of Mattakeesett and Satuckett. The Wampanoag in the south and the Massachusett in the north argued over the ownership of the land, traversed by the Tunk or Tunck pathway. The first English settlers arrived in the mid-1600s, with some records showing 1632. Before Hanson, it was the West Parish of Pembroke, known as Tunk. Pembroke itself was included in the land of Duxbury. The town of Hanson was named for Senator Alexander Contee Hanson of Baltimore, who was a newspaperman and later congressman who was outspoken against the War of 1812. Although smaller industry grew in Hanson, it was primarily an agrarian town. Farms and cranberry bogs are sources of income today. The town is bordered by Abington, Rockland, Hanover, Pembroke, Halifax and East Bridgewater. Hanson consists of much fresh water, including Saw Mill River, White Oak Brook, Poor Meadow Brook, Maquan Pond and the Rocky Run River. The Bay Circuit Trail cuts through town, even crossing the property of the former tuberculosis sanitarium, Plymouth County Hospital. Also known as Cranberry Specialty Hospital, it was in use from 1919 to 1992 and contained services such as occupational and physical therapies. It was built in an Italianate style with a deep red roof. After years of neglect, the former hospital was torn down.

The Nathaniel Thomas Mill in Hanson harkens back to a bygone era. *Author's photo.*

The Needles Lodge was the summer home of Albert Burrage, a Boston industrialist. It was built in 1906, destroyed by fire a year later and then rebuilt in 1908. Today, it is part of Camp Kiwanee. Another famous landmark is the Bonney Hill fire tower, dating from 1909, which went operational four years later. This hill is one of the tallest in the county. (Manomet Hill in Plymouth is the tallest.) Hanson's town hall is of spectacular design; it resides on Liberty Street and was built in 1872. The town hall has served as the site of civic functions for years. For history you can experience, dine at the Olde Hitching Post at 48 Spring Street in Hanson. Guests eat in the dining room or tavern of this circa 1810 farmhouse converted to a restaurant.

Hanson's settled history begins in the 1600s. In 1662, thirty-four individuals, led by Josiah Winslow of Marshfield, purchased land from Sachem Wampatuck. In what was known as the Major's Purchase, one thousand acres were left to George Wampy and the son of Wampatuck. The delineation of land was spurred by John Thomson of Middleborough, John Soule of Duxbury and Nathaniel Thomas of Marshfield.

Hanson's Schoolhouse No. 4 is in the National Register of Historic Places and operated by the historical society. The Nathaniel Thomas Mill, located across the street from the town hall, was re-created in 1976. Thomas bought 250 acres of land from the local Indigenous peoples. He dammed the Indian Head River and built a sawmill in the 1690s. This was followed in 1703 by a fishway that gave passage to the alewives on their annual run. It was patrolled to make sure that there was no illegal poaching. The West Parish Meetinghouse was incorporated in 1748 after members requested their own parish two years earlier. Additional early industries were carpentry, barrel making, a tannery and nail, shoe and tack making. In the 1800s, more small mills joined the others. Joseph White ran a successful carriage business. The oldest houses still standing date from the 1730s. Hanson's young men fought in wars starting with the French and Indian and continuing throughout the nation's military endeavors. The oldest cemetery in Hanson is Fern Hill Cemetery on High Street. The Civil War monument was originally located here, but it was moved to the town green. Throughout its history, Hanson has retained its small-town feel, even though housing sprawl has caught up with it, as it is now part of suburban Boston.

HALIFAX

"Incorporated 1734"

Similar to Hanson, Carver and Plympton, in the twenty-first century, Halifax still feels like a small town. Of the four, it has the most chain stores and suburban amenities. Conversely, agriculturally, it remains literally fruitful, and its town center retains much of its Old-World charm. Areas of the town were known for occupation by Indigenous peoples, with Monponsett Pond being the location of three sites. The name *Halifax* is derived from the town of the same name in England. Early English settlers arrived by 1669, but the town was not incorporated until 1734, with the establishment of the first church. Industry began in Halifax in 1728, but throughout the town's tenure, farming was at the forefront. The meetinghouse was erected in 1733, the first parsonage was built in 1739 and the current boundaries of the town were established in 1863. Schoolhouse No. 1 was at the corner of Monponsett and Plymouth Streets. It later became the first fire station and is now in the center of town. There were five districts with a school in each. The town center's appeal is quintessential New England, with the white Congregational church, town hall, green, cemetery and other historic buildings. The current Halifax Congregational Church was built in 1854. Standish Manor, also known as the Elms, was a prominent Halifax estate. The home, built in 1733, and outbuildings were situated on roughly seven hundred acres, including prime lakefront real estate on Monponsett Pond. It later became a school for girls. Industry in Halifax centered on a few mills, including a sawmill and woolen mill, and an ironworks.

The main industrial site, at the corner of Furnace and Elm Streets, burned down in 1848. This, coupled with the railroad arriving in Halifax in 1845, led to the decline of industrialization. The town has remained agrarian in nature, with cranberry harvesting historically and presently a major industry. Halifax is the birthplace of famed architect Alexander Parris. He is known for such buildings as the Pilgrim Hall Museum in Plymouth, the arsenal in Watertown and many lighthouses, from New York to Maine. The Halifax Central Cemetery is the final resting place of James J. Kilroy of the "Kilroy was here" graffiti (more about Kilroy in the "Former Military Holdings" chapter). All three of these South Shore towns had forays into industrialization but have been primarily rooted in agriculture.

CARVER

"Incorporated 1790"

Carver, named for the first governor of Plymouth Colony, John Carver, is best known today for three things: cranberries, jousting knights and Thomas the Tank Engine. It is home to the Edaville Family Amusement Park, which features Thomas Land, rides with Thomas and friends. Every fall, King Richard's Faire, a highly regarded renaissance fair, brings a bit of bawdy and chivalrous entertainment to the woods of Carver. Lastly, the little round cranberry put Carver on the map, harkening back to the time after industry dried up in town. Cranberry bogs are scattered throughout the land and turn the landscape of Carver a cranberry red each autumn.

The modern-day Carver's history dates back to 1790, the year it separated from Plympton and became its own town. Although the King Richard's Faire, a major seasonal attraction in town, dates to the 1500s, there is actual history in Carver from around 10,000 years ago. Uncovered in 1978, what is known as the Annasnappet Pond Site in North Carver was discovered as a highway renovation project was underway. The dig occurred at the site of

A cranberry bog in Carver. *Author's photo*.

a former cranberry bog, one that dated from 1886, and artifacts from 9000 BCE to 1000 CE were unearthed. Among the items found here were stone tools and stone flakes as well as a burial site. Although stone flakes may sound like a primitive cereal, in actuality they are fragments of stone that were often used for cutting. The traces of the first nomadic hunter-gatherer groups date from around 8000 BCE. The first permanent settlement in the area had remnants from about 7,500 years ago, including stone tools and even a burial site. The name *Annasnappet* translates to "at the source of the head of the brook." The period of inhabitation ranges from the late Paleoindian to the mid-period Woodland. Most of the artifacts date from the mid-Archaic age. In all, over 100,000 stone flakes were discovered and over 1,600 tools, including pestles, stone axes, spear points, sharpening stones and pieces of soapstone bowls. It is suggested that this collection is the largest of its kind in the northeastern United States.

During the early settlement of Carver by the colonists, iron ore was culled from town swamps, and wool and lumber were important products. One of the main sources of the bog iron was found at Sampson's Pond. In the 1730s, when Carver was still part of Plympton, one of the earliest iron furnaces was erected at Popes Point, which became a small village. Although rural, Carver has historically been composed of small villages. These include North Carver, previously known as Colchester and Lakenham, South Carver and East Carver, whose former names include Wenham. Wenham was also known for its iron furnace located on Wenham Brook, built in 1827. A proliferation of schoolhouses throughout the villages included the Carver Primary, Popes Point, Bates Pond, Wenham and South Carver schoolhouses.

The era of iron ore mining declined in the mid-nineteenth century, and cranberry farming rose in popularity in its place. The first cranberry crops were cultivated in the 1870s for export, even though records show that cranberries were eaten by the colonists. One of the most well-known of the cranberry growing areas was called the New Meadows, a natural five-hundred-acre cranberry bog. Harvesting the cranberries was difficult work. Part of the cranberry workforce were boys who would plunge into the freezing bog waters. As the cranberry crop rose in prominence, private ownership disputes of bogs arose, especially as this became big business in Carver. To expedite the industry, a railroad line connected the rural town to major metropolitan areas of Boston, New York City and Philadelphia. By 1900, 20 percent of all the cranberries grown in the United States were exported from Carver. Carver and cranberries have continued to be connected. Bogs are located throughout Carver even today. Cranberry giant Ocean Spray has a major facility in Carver, with its headquarters geographically close in Middleborough. Among the bogs and cranberry-related agritourism in Carver available for the public to visit are Fresh Meadows, Flax Pond Farms and Bensons Pond. (For more information, visit the database at www.cranberry.org.) A natural attraction popular with hikers, bikers and other outdoor enthusiasts is Myles Standish State Forest. Massachusetts's largest state forest is shared by Carver and Plymouth. For more information, see the chapter on Plymouth.

YOUR GUIDE TO HISTORY

King Richard's Faire

235 Carver Avenue, Carver, MA 02330
508-866-5391, www.kingrichardsfaire.net, Admission $34

Although history is the focus of this book, the history that is depicted at King Richard's Faire harkens back to the days of knights, kings and princesses, all

Savery Avenue in Carver is the first divided highway in the nation. *Author's photo.*

the way to the 1500s. Here family-friendly entertainment abounds. Expect a constant array of shows, including musical and theatrical performances. Other special events such as a big cat display or a jousting contest are held throughout the weekend days of the faire. Enjoy a giant turkey leg and partake in the revelry. The annual event takes place on weekends in September and October at the fairgrounds located at 235 Main Street in Carver. The buildings are permanent fixtures in the woods and the re-created village. Look for the Tudor building marking the entrance.

Savery Avenue

Carver, MA 02330

This is a small loop road off Main Street. To the uneducated, it may seem like just another bucolic lane in this section of the South Shore. In actuality, this is America's first divided highway. The two sides of the road are halved by a line of trees. It dates from 1861.

Edaville Family Amusement Park

5 Pine Street, Carver, MA 02330
508-866-8190, www.edaville.com, Admission $37 (adult price),

Smaller theme parks have shuttered all throughout New England, while larger Six Flags–type parks draw the crowds. Edaville was in danger of becoming only a memory when it transformed itself recently and added the only Thomas Land (home of Thomas the Tank Engine and friends) in the country. The park began in 1947 by Ellis D. Atwood (EDA) as a tourist train. Atwood culled a collection of narrow-gauge locomotives from various defunct rail lines in Maine. The train followed a five-and-a-half mile loop around his property and passed by cranberry bogs which are stunning in the autumn dressed in the vibrant shade of red. Through various ownership, the park ceased operations in 1992. After delays, it reopened in 1999. Along with the train ride, the park featured small amusement rides and a petting zoo. One event which occurred during the months of November and December was the Edaville Festival of Lights. The train passed through the park and environs aglow in a swath of Christmas lights.

With the addition of Thomas Land in 2015, the park spruced itself up and draws hearty crowds. The train ride has been shortened in length; now it is a twenty-minute loop on a two-mile track that circles the property. In addition to the narrow-gauge locomotives, Thomas also pulls the train. The train ride is the highlight of the park.

The rest of the park includes carnival-type rides such as the Tilt-o-Whirl, Ferris wheel and merry-go-round. Edaville is best for younger children, since the park lacks fast and jaw-dropping roller coasters of major amusement park brands. Upon entering through the gate, Edaville's version of Main Street greets visitors with stores and places to get food. There is a Victorian village to walk through, and it is bedecked for Christmas. The Festival of Lights is still a beloved annual tradition. The grounds are well manicured, with a pond as a focal point of the property. During the summer, Dino Land includes a walking trail in which animatronic dinosaurs roar behind each corner. Edaville is a premier family fun destination on the South Shore.

10

ABINGTON

"MANAMOOSKEAGIN"

Abington's history is inextricably linked to that of Rockland and Whitman. This is not only because these towns share the same predominant manufacturing of shoes, but because all were the same town until 1874. That is the year Rockland broke away to form its own municipality, and Whitman did the same a year later, although Whitman was originally known as South Abington. Being a part of a bigger town was nothing new. Abington itself was part of Bridgewater, a purchase that was made by Myles Standish—the Bridgewater Purchase with local Native Americans as an extension of Duxbury.

Prior to English occupation, the region of Abington was land that was on the border between that of the Wampanoag to the south and the Massachusett to the north. The region was known in the Algonquin language as Manamooskeagin, which translates as the "great green place of shaking grass." This name even adorns the Abington town seal. Beaver were ubiquitous in the region, and two of the major waterways were known as upper and lower Beaver Brooks. A Native American trail, known as the Satucket Path, ran through it. Andrew Ford, from Weymouth, was the first English settler to the region in 1668. Abington broke away from Bridgewater to form its own town in 1712. Citizens had vied for sovereignty six years earlier in 1706, but the request was not granted. Reverend Samuel Brown, originally from Newbury, Massachusetts, arrived, scheduled to become minister. Through this action, Abington was granted its own

Crossing into Island Grove Park. *Author's photo.*

charter. Abington was named in homage of the Countess of Abingdon in England, Anne Bertie, who appointed Governor Dudley to his role in the Massachusetts Bay Colony.

Abington's first major industry was that of lumber. Trees felled here were turned into lumber and used in the construction of many homes and even in the shipbuilding industry on the nearby North River. Lumber from Abington was even used as the floorboards of the USS *Constitution*. The first sawmills in town began operating around the year 1700, with tanneries following in 1710. The first schoolhouse was built in 1732, and by 1755, the town was divided into five different districts, all punctuated by a schoolhouse. The current United Church of Christ sits near the original meetinghouse. Nearby was a clay pit in which colonial-era pottery was created.

Shoe manufacturing was the most important industry to Abington. The first shoe manufacturers were part of a small cottage industry in town. Throughout the nineteenth century, many people, including the Irish, moved to work here. Shoe companies such as Crossett, Arnold and Turner, among many others, called Abington home. By 1850, Abington housed thirty-six boot and shoe factories. With the advent of the Civil War and the need for soldier footwear, the shoes of Abington were in constant demand. In the 1930s, the Great Depression witnessed the fading of the Abington shoe industry.

The Crossett factory building still stands at 10 Railroad Street. Most recently, it housed the New England Art Publishers. Currently vacant, there is speculation that the wooden factory is slated for rehabilitation into residential housing similar to that of the Emerson Shoe Lofts in Rockland or the Bostonian Shoe Lofts in Whitman. The Arnold Shoe Factory has also been renovated. The brick factory is located at 200 Wales Street and houses businesses of all kinds. Both of these are in the North Abington section close to the border of Rockland. North Abington was also the scene of an 1893 riot between railroad workers and the townspeople. The Old Colony Railroad rumbled through this section of town north to south beginning in 1845. The Town of Abington wanted to install a streetcar system, but it was met with staunch opposition by the railroad company. A clash ensued between the two parties. The streetcar was eventually installed, and as if extending an olive branch to the railroad, the Richardsonian Romanesque North Abington Railroad Station was built. North Abington would see direct service on the Old Colony. Today, this railway is part of the MBTA's commuter rail system. The former North Abington Depot is now the Abington Depot Restaurant and Bar.

Since Abington is synonymous with shoes, it may be a surprise that the Buffum automobile was also manufactured here. Herbert H. Buffum, originally in the shoe business, switched over to the automotive industry. The Buffum automobile was an early American car. Although exact dates have been obscured by the sands of time, its production lasted only a brief while in the early years of the twentieth century.

As superhighways were built to connect the South Shore to the Boston area, Abington, similar to many other towns, transformed itself from a former industrial town to a bedroom community of Boston. Today, Abington is mainly residential, with former testaments of its past that are hidden in plain sight. Former shoemaking factories still exist, as do homes from Abington's first century as an independent town, the 1700s. Today, the town is composed of modern neighborhoods and businesses that revolve around the major routes of 58, 18, 139 and 123. Abington doesn't have a downtown in the traditional sense. What it lacks in that category, it makes up with parks and green space.

The Civil War memorial arch at Island Grove Park. *Author's photo.*

YOUR GUIDE TO HISTORY

Island Grove Park

Entrance off of Park Avenue and Lake Street, Abington, MA 02351
www.friendsofislandgrove.com

For most visitors, Island Grove Park provides a welcome respite from the hustle and bustle of its three major roads, all located close by, and the chugging of the train, which seems to frequently pass by. Entering the park from the series of spaces on Park Street, the visitor encounters paths lined with pine trees. The paths meander through a small woodland with a pond in the middle. This pond is used as a camp area in the summer. On the western side of the public parcel is an arch that was dedicated on the two hundredth anniversary of the town in 1912 in tribute to the soldiers who fought in the Civil War. The arch leads to a causeway over a dammed portion of the Shumatuscacant River (the name means "lower beaver brook"). The park is popular with runners, fishermen and dog walkers, most of whom do not know the importance of this piece of land.

This park was an active location in the abolition movement of Massachusetts. The annual gatherings known as the August 1st meetings (named for the date of meeting) took place here and were led by famed Boston abolitionist William Lloyd Garrison. The park was mentioned on numerous occasions in his influential newspaper, the *Liberator*. The annual events were well attended, but with the advent of the Old Colony Railroad reaching Abington, attendance skyrocketed. These meetings took place until the Civil War. In addition to this, the site also housed industry and contained an amusement park. Today, it is simply a pretty, secluded place to take a walk. Island Grove was added to the National Register of Historic Places in 2002. The parking area for Island Grove is on Park Avenue and Lake Street.

11

PEMBROKE

"1712"

The region of Pembroke, with its abundance of freshwater ponds and rivers, was known as fishing grounds for the Massachusett and the Wampanoag, both local Native American tribes. The region of Pembroke, on the whole, was known as Mattakeesett, while the area of Pembroke nearest to the fresh water was known as Nemassakeesett, translated as "place of much fish" by the Massachusett. Mattakeesett translates as "fertile place between the lakes where the corn grows best" or "worn out planting lands," depending on the source. The river herring, plentiful in the streams and ponds, as the fish "run" or swim upstream from the Atlantic Ocean to the ponds of Pembroke, have been a source of sustenance for the Indigenous peoples and the English settlers. (Fishing for river herring is not allowed today in an effort to restore the abundance of fish to their natural habitat.)

The land that would become Pembroke was acquired by the English from Sachem Josiah Wampatuck. Upon settlement by the English, this region was part of Duxbury. The first settlers to the area were Dolor Davis and Robert Barker from Scituate. These early residents chose the Nemassakeesett region, nearer to the sources of water. Named after the town of Pembroke in Wales, Pembroke was incorporated in 1712. Today's town borders are very different from that period. A two-mile district of Scituate became North Pembroke close to the North River. Part of Marshfield was absorbed into the town of Pembroke. Place names such as Crookertown and Fosterville were once villages within the town. The West

The First Church in Pembroke. *Author's photo.*

Parish of Pembroke, also known as Tunk, was established as Hanson in 1820. For a small town, Pembroke is multifaceted. Although it is agrarian due to the proximity of rivers, industry played a major role as well. The Pembroke Iron Works was established in 1720. The earliest mills dated from 1690. Pembroke was known widely as a shipbuilding community on the North River. The shipbuilding industry existed for almost two hundred years, between the years of 1678 and 1871. In total, roughly 1,025 ships were manufactured at the yards on the North River in Pembroke and environs. The shipyards here included Brick Kiln Yard, Seabury Point, Job's Landing, Turner's Yard and Macy's. Among the famous ships constructed on the North River in Pembroke was the *Beaver*, best known as the boat from which the Sons of Liberty deposited the tea into Boston Harbor, at Brick Kiln Yard, and the *Maria*, which adorns the town seal. Furnace Pond, a point of origin for the transient river herring, was once the site of an iron furnace erected in 1702. In terms of agriculture, ponds were modified to grow cranberries, creating the still extant cranberry bogs. In the West Parish of Pembroke, later to be Hanson, Reverend Gad Hitchcock gave a sermon at the Old State House in Boston to influential leaders under King George III, among them General Gage. Pembroke was also active in the cause for abolition and home of the suffragette Lavinia Hatch (who was friends with Susan B. Anthony).

Pembroke was opened up to more visitors, who especially enjoyed the tranquil ponds with their cool water, as the railroad came to town. Pembroke had the distinction of being on the route between Whitman and Plymouth, which helped give rise to the summer resort area in Bryantville called Mayflower Grove. With accessibility from Boston, city dwellers ventured to Pembroke to beat the heat during the summer. With increasing traffic to and from town via the highway, Route 3, Pembroke became a bedroom community of Boston. The town's population of 18,358 in 2016 represents steady growth. With no major town center, twenty-first-century Pembroke is mostly residential, although it still hides in plain sight some very interesting historic sites and tales of its past.

YOUR GUIDE TO HISTORY

Route 36 and the Hobomock Inn

300 Center Street, Pembroke, MA 02359

Traveling State Road 36 from Route 14 in Pembroke Center to Route 106 in Halifax, a driver might wonder, why is this a state road? It's quite short, less than five and a half miles, and parallels the larger Route 58.

Pembroke is known for its many ponds. *Author's photo.*

Local lore states that controversial four-time Boston mayor and governor of Massachusetts from 1937 to 1939 James Michael Curley was the reason for this stretch of road being converted to a state road. The impetus was the Hobomock Inn, located at 300 Center Street. This was a favorite meeting place and drinking establishment for Curley and his political pals, some say even during Prohibition. Long before the era of GPS and Google Maps, Curley had the road deemed a state road so that it would be easier for his entourage to locate it. Additionally, given its state-maintained status, snow would be removed, making it available to Curley in any weather. The Hobomock Inn is gone. The current building has housed restaurants in recent years, including Oliveira's, Arrow, Lake Palace Chinese and the very appropriately named JM Curley's. The restaurant's back deck overlooks Hobomock Pond, which is in its backyard. Currently, the space is without a tenant. Some sources even mention Babe Ruth as a customer at this bar.

Mayflower Grove

When a Plymouth and Brockton Railway Company streetcar line was established between Whitman and Plymouth, more travelers discovered Pembroke. Through this railway, the coast was easier to access for those living in landlocked towns. Pembroke, in capitalizing on its location roughly halfway between the two termini, became the site of an amusement park in 1901. It was named Mayflower Grove, located on School Street on the banks of Little Sandy Pond in the Bryantville section of Pembroke. The park operated between the turn of the twentieth century and roughly 1940. Many attractions were there for visitors to enjoy. As the automobile competed with the streetcar as the primary mechanism for travel, Mayflower Grove's parking lots filled up with cars, many from out of state. The park offered a hotel, a restaurant, a dance hall, a carousel, games, an open-air theater and a pool hall. Clambakes were a popular celebratory meal here. Canoes were available, and fireworks were set off from a raft in the pond. Weddings were held, and popular local big bands played here. There were greased pig–catching contests for children. In the park's later years, a mini-golf course was added, and Miss America even graced the stage at Mayflower Grove. Closer in years to its demise, the park was radically altered, with many of the older attractions refitted to accommodate a movie house and a roller-skating rink. In this capacity, the park did not last long, as it closed its doors around 1940. The land was sold to make way for a housing development. When one drives through Bryantville on Route 27, no traces of the Grove's past remain, save for the pond. As access from the city became easier, Pembroke became a vacation destination with its many cool ponds attracting those who ventured from Boston to escape scorching summer days in the city.

Pembroke Resolves and the First Church of Pembroke

105 Center Street, Pembroke, MA 02359
781-293-2584, www.firstchurchinpembroke.org

Inspired by the Boston Committee of Correspondence in November 1772, a group of Pembroke residents banded together to write the "Pembroke Resolves," which was the first act of public discourse against the British Crown. The document outlined the reasons for the separation of the colonies against the mother country. It was written by John Turner, who led the Pembroke Committee of Correspondence, along with Abel Stetson, Jeremiah Hill and Captain Seth Hatch. Patriotism ran deep in Pembroke. The Resolves were established at the First Church in Pembroke on December 28, 1772. The current house of worship dates from 1837, but the site had been a meetinghouse since 1712.

John Turner House

369 Washington Street, Pembroke, MA 02359
781-293-9083 (Pembroke Historical Society), www.pembrokehistoricalsociety.org

Turner was the leader of Pembroke's Committee of Correspondence. He was a mill owner whose building was located nearby. Turner was a fervent Patriot who held many offices in town, including clerk. He represented Pembroke in the Provincial Congress from 1772 to 1782 and fought in the American Revolution. He was born in 1712 and died in 1794. His house sits at 369 Washington Street, at the corners of Routes 53 and 14, currently in a state of dilapidation behind a Sunoco gas station. The records of this home are conflicting. Some sources have the Federal home dating from John Turner's lifetime in 1760, while others say the point of origin is around 1820, as it was built for a Turner descendant, Paul Turner, with the possibility that a section of it, or lumber, was used from an earlier abode. The land was in the Turner family for years, and houses were situated on this parcel before the Turner home. During an earlier rehabilitation of the home, beams from 1720 have been discovered. Today, it sits in a sad state of neglect, although the town has recently undertaken an emergency stabilization of the building. The hope is to restore it again to functional conditions. The historical society is deciding what the function of this building will be.

The Whaler Beaver

The North River and the towns alongside it were known for the shipbuilding industry. Pembroke was no exception. One of the most famous boats built in Pembroke was the whaler *Beaver*, although it has been known by posterity less for its whaling and more for what was expelled from its deck. The ship was constructed at Ichabod Thomas's Brick Kiln Shipyard in the early 1770s. Commissioned by Joseph Rotch, a Quaker from Nantucket, its first expedition in 1773 brought whale oil from the island to London. On its return trip, it shuttled 112 tea chests courtesy of the East India Company. It stayed in port in the Fort Point Channel of Boston for two weeks, as the crew was stricken by smallpox. The ship was in port in Boston when it was commandeered by the Sons of Liberty and its tea ransacked and thrown overboard.

Uljas Koitto Temperance Society Traditional Finnish Sauna

83 Suomi Road, Pembroke, MA 02359
781-293-8434, www.uktshome.com, Admission $40

Buried in the grove of pine trees on the banks of Furnace Pond is a unique South Shore gem that has a long history in its own right. Located on Suomi Road, which translates to "Finnish," is the spa of the Uljas Koitto Temperance Society, which began in 1892 in retaliation to the power of the drink. Alcohol is still not allowed here, for the sauna promotes pureness. Many Finns migrated to the South Shore to work in the quarries of Quincy in the late 1800s. The sauna—not in the twenty-first-century sense of the word, which is often used as an addendum to a spa with other pampering services—dates from 1927 and consists of two cabin-like buildings powered by burning wood. The temperature inside the men's and women's saunas reaches 220 degrees Fahrenheit. After the sauna-goer reaches an optimum level of warmth (or an unbearable swelter), they exit the sauna and take a dip in Furnace Pond, only a few steps away. (A hole is cut through the ice to allow visitors to plunge during the snow-covered months). In addition to the two saunas is a lodge, acquired by the society in 1927, dating from the turn of the twentieth century. It was a former hunting lodge; the porch is now used as a cafeteria with coffee and pastries. Admission is charged, cash only, and it is run entirely by volunteers.

12

KINGSTON

"BRIG INDEPENDENCE"

Kingston was settled as the northern section of Plymouth in 1620 upon the Separatists' arrival. Prior to that, it was the land of the Wampanoag. Kingston as a separate community was settled later than its neighbors of Plymouth and Duxbury, with official incorporation granted in 1726. The architecture in the center of town around Main, Evergreen and Summer Streets is a testament to its growth during this period. This section of town features stately homes and municipal buildings, many dating from the eighteenth and nineteenth centuries. The fourteen-acre tract of land that became the town center was awarded by Major John Bradford, who owned much of the acreage that would become Kingston. The beauty of Kingston center is best shown at the annual Luminary Night held in mid-December. Many of the roads that make up the heart of the community are heavily trafficked today, as Main Street is also Route 106, which connects the coastal South Shore to interior towns of Pembroke and Hanson. Summer Street is Route 3A, which runs north to south hugging the coast and paralleling the major highway, Route 3.

On Luminary Night, the town center is devoid of traffic, and luminaries, which are basically candles placed in bags, line both sides of the road throughout this neighborhood. The effect is mesmerizing, but even better, the pedestrian is allowed to take in the architectural beauty of the town center without the ever-present rush of automobiles zapping the tranquility from the moment. Geographically, a major feature of Kingston is the Jones

The Major John Bradford House dates from 1714 and now is a museum. *Author's photo.*

River, which spans the town from west to east. Its source is Silver Lake in Kingston, and it pours into the Atlantic Ocean in Kingston Bay.

During the era of the Pilgrims, the land that would become Kingston was best known as the home of Governor William Bradford. The area was known as the northern precinct of Plymouth. It was not until 1717 that a group of 41 residents banded together and petitioned to form their own town. This officially occurred in 1726 since an appropriate church leader had to be found before incorporation. When township status was granted, there were 550 residents living within its borders. Much of the early land was donated by Major John Bradford, including that of the First Parish Church; the Training Green from 1720; the Faunce School on Green Street; the Old Burial Ground, consecrated in 1717; and the home for minister Joseph Stacy of the church at the intersection of Summer and Main Streets. The area was given the moniker of Jones River Village. Among the other architectural gems in the neighborhood are the First Parish Meeting House (now the First Parish Unitarian Church) on Main Street, Evergreen Cemetery and the Frederic C. Adams Library (now the Adams Center, which holds civic functions). The town boundaries of Kingston were finally established in 1857 when the Rocky Nook section was annexed by Kingston from Duxbury.

The industry was reliant on the town's geographic features, most notably its water. The Jones River provided manufacturing such as boat building and nail and tack factories. The most famous ship constructed at the Jones River was the Revolutionary-era USS *Independence*, and it is featured on the town seal of Kingston. The shipyard known as the Jones River Landing has been in the longest constant operation of any boatyard in America. Wharves lined the coastline at Rocky Nook. Here the system of ropes and masts, known as the rigging, was constructed after the ships were built at the Jones River. At the industry's height, the three largest ship manufacturers built hundreds of boats in total. The shipbuilding industry would come to a close by 1874. Other industries included harvesting ice, farming and factory work. Other neighborhoods sprang up, including Wapping, Triphammer and Stony Brook. The Cobb and Drew tack factory was a major employer, and in the early twentieth century, there were ten such nail and tack factories in town. Given Kingston's proximity to Cordage Park in Plymouth, workers lived in Kingston. A trolley line was connected to Kingston from Plymouth to provide transportation to the mill. Rocky Nook became a summer resort village with cottages in proximity to the ocean. Kingston's identity drastically changed in the 1960s with the advent of Route 3. The town went from sleepy to suburban, as the highway connected Kingston to Boston and environs. The population boom increased when the Massachusetts Bay Transit Authority extended the commuter rail service to Kingston in 1997, utilizing the old Old Colony Railroad lines. As of 2017, there were roughly 13,500 residents in Kingston.

YOUR GUIDE TO HISTORY

Luminary Night

Luminary Night is an annual tradition that takes place on a Saturday night in mid-December. It is the town's holiday celebration; the neighborhood holds an open house, with goodies served at the town's first firehouse, the Surprise Hose Company, on Main Street. The streets are closed to automobile traffic, and both sides of the road are lined with luminaries. It provides a magical effect, as the true majesty of Kingston's architecture is on display, draped in the colors of the holiday. The annual event dates back to 1986. Entertainment and crafts are found at

An example of the stately architecture that makes up the historic district of Kingston. *Author's photo.*

the Reed Center. The library holds events, and the churches are open, often featuring musical performances. The whole neighborhood has a festive atmosphere, aglow in luminary candles. The town tree is lit as the centerpiece of the evening, and the Boy Scouts hold a Christmas tree raffle. The Surprise Hose Company (on Main Street) is a historic fire station, Kingston's first, that dates from 1925. The former station is now a museum. The luminaries are displayed on Main Street, Evergreen Street, Summer Street and the side roads in between.

Jones River

The Jones River can be seen flowing through Kingston

The unassuming seven-and-a-half-mile Jones River, which flows through the town of Kingston, paints a pretty picture. It was named for the captain of the *Mayflower*, Master Christopher Jones. Although picturesque today, this river was once a hotbed for shipbuilding on the South Shore. The freshwater source begins in Silver Lake, which was once known as the Jones River Pond, to the ocean in Kingston Bay. The lake is one of the largest in Massachusetts at eighty feet deep and roughly a mile in size. It is the source of drinking water for the city of Brockton.

Shipbuilding began in the early 1700s on the Jones River. Boat building flourished here during the 1700s and 1800s. The Drew family, who moved to Kingston from Duxbury in 1713, was a stronghold in the shipbuilding industry in town from the early eighteenth century to the 1870s. The first brig manufactured in the newly chartered town of Kingston was the appropriately named *Kingston* in 1726. The *Independence*, the most well-known ship built in Kingston and featured on the town seal, was constructed by the Drews. Ships such as those manufactured on the Jones River gave way to larger craft such as merchant vessels and steamships. The primary shipbuilding era in Kingston ended with the advent of these larger boats by 1874. Although most of the industry stopped in 1874, Jones River Landing is known for being the oldest shipyard in continuous use in the country.

Baclajau

Jones River Village Historical Society
Landing Road, Kingston, MA 02364
781-585-6300, www.jrvhs.org

George Shiverick was a Cape Cod–born boat builder descended from a lineage of boat builders extraordinaire. George was best known for the racing boats that he designed called catboats. He moved to Kingston in 1895 and lived on land that is now part of the Jones River Landing (which is why his boat shop is still there). His reputation as a premier boat builder spread, and he even designed one that belonged to Franklin D. Roosevelt. In his lifetime, he constructed 232 boats. A one-hundred-year-old catboat, the *Baclajau*, was restored by the Jones River Village Historical Society. The rehabilitated boat's maiden voyage took place on August 26, 2017, as it set sail at the landing. Restoring such an old vessel is always exciting, but in this case, Shiverick destroyed most of his plans, so the ability to take a Shiverick creation and make it seaworthy was extraordinarily special.

Old Burying Ground

Main Street, Kingston, MA 02364

The first graveyard in town was part of the land donation given by Major John Bradford. Notable Kingstonians are interred here, including those with last names of Bradford, Faunce and Adams. This is the final resting place of Major John Bradford and located adjacent to the First Parish Church.

Major John Bradford Homestead

50 Landing Road, Kingston, MA 02364
781-585-6300, www.jrvhs.org

Major John Bradford was the grandson of *Mayflower* passenger Governor William Bradford. He owned much land in the area that would become Kingston. The original section of his house is speculated by some historians to date from 1675; others deem it 1714. The Bradford house is the site of the

Jones River Village Historical Society and operates as its headquarters and a museum. It offers Sunday breakfasts during the summer months. A circa 1798 threshing barn and a beautiful, well-tended garden are also on site. Bradford was a representative to the General Assembly as well as a military leader of Plymouth.

Evergreen Cemetery

21 Green Street, Kingston, MA 02364
781-585-4507, www.kingstonevergreencemetery.com

Evergreen is a beautiful garden cemetery reminiscent of Mount Auburn Cemetery in Watertown, Massachusetts (albeit on a smaller scale). It dates from 1853 and has roads and paths that snake about. The campus includes a serene pond and a chapel. Gravestones are scattered, not in the typical rows of most graveyards. The cemetery is located on Green and Evergreen Streets. Word of caution: it is still an active burial ground.

Forty-Second Parallel Marker

Near the intersection of Loring Street and Parks Street

On Loring Street, close to the intersection of Parks Street near the Duxbury border, is a marker delineating this line of latitude. The imaginary line travels right through Kingston.

13

HANOVER

"INCORPORATED JUNE 14, 1721"

Hanover is typical of many of the interior towns in the South Shore region in that the land once belonged to one of its neighbors. During its early years, it was mainly agricultural in nature with small industry appearing later, including the manufacture of shoes and tacks. It was home to a prominent shipbuilding enterprise and, in more recent times, has become a residential bedroom town of Boston. Just like every town in this book, though, it has its own unique features, both historical and natural. Its history includes the forging of the anchor for "Old Ironsides," the construction of the ship that is the emblem of Old Spice and the manufacture of fireworks and munitions during the twentieth century.

The first colonist to arrive in what would become Hanover was William Barstow, in 1649. Barstow's settlement was in proximity to the North River. (Hanover was the western part of Scituate.) Barstow designed a bridge over the North River, and it was one of the earliest bridges built over this waterway. Barstow operated a successful shipyard near today's Washington Street Bridge, and the Barstow Forge manufactured anchors.

Hanover did not become its own town until June 14, 1727. The speculation is that Hanover was named in tribute to King George, who died during the same month as the incorporation of the town. A more fitting name, such as Georgetown, would have been appropriate. (Georgetown, Massachusetts, was not incorporated until the next century.) King George (of Britain) was

Luddam's Ford, once a site of manufacturing, is now a serene park. *Jaclyn Lamothe.*

also the Electorate of Hanover, and he was born in Hanover, Germany. Hanover, Massachusetts, was named in homage to the German city but still with close affiliation to the mother country, England.

After Hanover's incorporation in 1727, the first meetinghouse was built the following year. Settlements arose along Third Herring Brook and on the banks of the Drinkwater River at West Hanover, North Hanover, Hanover Four Corners and Hanover Center.

Early Hanover's existence was marked by agriculture and lumber. Trees were felled to be used as lumber in the construction of houses and barns. Soon small mills were used to grind corn and other such subsistent products. Hanover was never the industrial force of Weymouth or Abington, for it was heavily rural. It did have some bigger industrial sites within the town, such as the Clapp Rubber Mill. Tack and shoe factories were also here. Charles Beach Russell and Rodolphus C. Waterman, both of Hanover, filed a patent for a nail or tack-making machine in 1898.

In the twentieth century, the National Fireworks Factory was the largest employer in town. Its history is detailed in the chapter on military history;

in addition to pyrotechnics, the factory also produced munitions. Today, Hanover is a mostly residential town with many mid-twentieth-century developments, although Colonial and Cape Cod–style homes from the eighteenth century can still be seen. Even though Washington Street, or Route 53, is mainly full of commercial enterprises, traces of the old villages of Hanover still remain. The center of town is located near the intersection of Main and Hanover Streets (Route 139). The town hall, library, First Congregational Church and cemetery are all located here. Assinippi, which is located on the Hanover/Norwell border, is mostly defined by strip mall shops. Although the town is mostly residential and commercial, Hanover has many preserved green spaces, including the Firehouse Loop Trail and the Morrill Allen Phillips Wildlife Sanctuary (behind Fire Station Number 5, which is now the Museum of Firefighting and is operated by the historical society), the Fireworks Property and the Indian Head Trail. Many of these are hidden gems that need a little digging to uncover. The trail system is large; many connect with one another.

Hanover Four Corners, the intersection of Broadway and Washington Streets, is often overlooked. The neighborhood's quaintness is palpable. It is only a short distance from Routes 53 and 139 but has character, while the main roads remain nondescript. Dating from 1808 and relocated from the town center, the former Hanover Academy, now an antique store, is a well-preserved nineteenth-century civic building. This was a popular stopover for stagecoaches en route to Boston or Plymouth, and two hotels were even located in this small village center. It lost its vitality when the main road was rerouted to the current Route 53 in the mid-twentieth century.

Hanover's history is congruent with that of the North River. For one, the North River provides the southern boundary of the town, separating it from Pembroke and Hanson. The shipbuilding industry on the North River was known far and wide.

Luddam's Ford on the Indian Head River, a main tributary of the North River, was the site of the construction of the anchor used on the ship USS *Constitution*, known colloquially as "Old Ironsides." Luddam's Ford has a unique history, detailed later. Anchor manufacture was a major industry in Hanover, with the most famous product used on the famed Old Ironsides. Another famous ship with Hanover ties is the *Grand Turk*. It was constructed at Barstow's Two Oaks shipyard during the American Revolution in 1781 as a privateer built for Salem's Elias Hasket Derby. The *Grand Turk* is best known as the logo of the Old Spice brand.

Even though Hanover was closely linked to agriculture in its early days and housing in more recent times, the industry it did have has had a lasting effect, albeit with negative reverberations still being felt today. The native river herring and shad have long been faced with a series of dams and other obstructions to their natural migratory path. Fishing is a popular sport on the rivers. Fishing for river herring is illegal, but eating any of the other bounty culled from these waters could prove harmful for human consumption. The National Fireworks Company used nearby Factory Pond as a dumping site for refuse and waste, and toxic levels of mercury are still found in the river today. In 2018, a fisherman, instead of a trout tugging at his line, reeled in an unexploded ordnance. As of this writing, the area has been shut down as a conservation area due to the detonation of explosives, even though production ceased during the Vietnam War years. Local residents speak of hearing loud explosions due to the controlled detonation. The Clapp Rubber Factory, also located on the Indian Head River, also polluted the waterways. Although pretty to look at, Hanover's rivers still need remediation.

YOUR GUIDE TO HISTORY

The Museum of Firefighting

1095 Broadway, Hanover, MA 02339
781-826-9575, www.hanoverhistoricalsociety.com

The Museum of Firefighting on Broadway is operated by the Hanover Historical Society in a former firehouse. The fire station was established in 1887. The building was originally the paint shop of Morrill Allen Phillips (for whom the abutting park is named). He was a lawyer and in the tack industry. In 1911, the South Hanover Fire Association (formed a year earlier) bought the building for use as its firehouse. It was in use until 1993, serving as a community center hosting grange meetings, dances and other functions. In 2000, it reopened as a museum. The museum details the history of firefighting in Hanover and houses artifacts related to the National Fireworks Company.

A view of Hanover Town Hall. *Jaclyn Lamothe.*

Stetson House

514 Hanover Street, Hanover, MA 02339
781-826-9575, www.hanoverhistoricalsociety.com

The Stetson House, built in 1716, is the headquarters of the Hanover Historical Society. Four generations of Stetsons lived in the Colonial home. The home and headquarters also is a museum that features period furnishings and displays related to the history of Hanover. The museum is located at 514 Hanover Street. Look for the yellow Colonial home.

Luddam's Ford Park

Elm Street, Hanover, MA 02339

This park off Elm Street is located on the banks near where the Indian Head and North Rivers converge. Today a picturesque place to paddle, picnic, fish or hike, it was once a highly successful industrial complex dating from the town's earliest days. The origin of the name *Luddam's Ford* is an entertaining historical tidbit. James Luddam, a guide to the area, carried Governor John Winthrop on his back while crossing this river on a journey from Plymouth. Winthrop wrote about it in his diary. From then on, it was known as Luddam's Ford. Remnants of the former industry are visible, including the old dam, stone bridge and fish ladder. The first industry at this site was a sawmill. In 1704, the Bardin Iron Forge was established, followed by the Curtis Anchor Forge, which produced 250 tons of anchors a year. The USS *Constitution*'s anchor was forged here in 1797. In 1873, the old Curtis buildings were completely renovated as the site of the Eugene Clapp Rubber Factory. The rubber factory grew on both sides of the river, in Hanover and Pembroke.

Today's Luddam's Ford Park is simply a pretty park that is worth exploring. It connects with the Indian Head River Trail, the path totaling about four miles in length. It is a scenic place to picnic or enjoy an outdoor activity.

14

COHASSET

"DISCOVERED 1614, PRECINCT 1717, TOWN 1770"

Cohasset was the site of Quonohasset, a village of the Massachusett tribe. The Algonquin word means "long rocky place." Geographically, the town is situated due east of Hingham, farther down the coast of the South Shore. The early history of Cohasset is tied to that of its neighbor, since from Hingham's settlement in 1635 to Cohasset's separate incorporation in 1770, Cohasset was part of Hingham. It was originally known as Conohasset. (The area was "discovered" by Captain John Smith in 1614.) The land that would become Cohasset was divvied up in 1670 into roughly one-square-mile-size lots along the town's main street. This eastern section of the town of Hingham vied for its own meetinghouse in 1713. In 1717, this was granted to the townspeople and known as Hingham's Second Precinct. Early industries in town included farming and lumber. Nehemiah Hobart was the first minister of Cohasset and was the grandson of the founder of Hingham, Peter Hobart. During the War of 1812, in June 1814, the British burned a sloop in the area of Cohasset Harbor. As the decades progressed, the town's industries turned toward the sea. Cod fishing was a major source of livelihood until the year 1840. Fleets would leave from the Cohasset Harbor and fish in the Grand Banks off Newfoundland. Up to sixty fishing vessels were harbored in Cohasset, and wharves lined the harbor. The lumber industry provided wood to manufacture the boats. Along with fishing came the other businesses that were necessary to boat building, including blacksmithing, barrel making, salt

The First Parish in Cohasset punctuates the town green. *Author's photo*.

procurement and the manufacture of sails. As the fishing industry faded, the harbor was still alive with boats, albeit ones built for pleasure. Today's harbor is quiet. It is a picturesque cove.

Although agriculture was important, given Cohasset's proximity to the sea, the town has had a long history related to the Atlantic Ocean. The coast of Cohasset is not sandy like that of Marshfield or Plymouth; instead, it is rough and rocky and the cause of many a shipwreck. In 1894, Cohasset's yacht club was founded. The famed yachtsman Captain Aubrey Crocker was from the town. He was part of the crew that won the America's Cup on the *Puritan* and raced on a team out of New York City. As time went on, summer residents filled Cohasset's coastline. Its rock-strewn shoreline is dangerous for those at sea who are unfamiliar with it but provides astonishing views for those on land. Summer cottage dwellers picked streets such as Jerusalem Road and Atlantic Avenue for their proximity to water. (The cottages have been turned into multimillion-dollar homes.) To diminish the danger of the rocky granite coast, the Minot's Ledge Light, located on the Scituate and Cohasset border, was erected in 1860 after the first one was built in 1850 and burned a year later.

Unlike many towns along the South Shore, Cohasset was mostly immune to the advancements in mechanization. There were a few exceptions. Among them were an ironworks dating from 1704 and a mill from 1792 that burned in 1862, as well as the Hagerty Company and Kennedy Antenna in more recent years.

In the twenty-first century, Cohasset exudes a bygone charm. It is a highly coveted destination for homeowners, and rightly so, since the town is only about sixteen miles from Boston as the crow flies. To reach Route 3, one must drive through Hingham or other South Shore towns; Cohasset's downtown has remained independent. Yes, on Route 3A (Chief Justice Cushing Highway) there is a series of strip malls, but the waterfront and downtown have been untouched by sprawl. Around the town common are mostly eighteenth-century homes, the town hall, three churches (two on the green and St. Stephen's near the far end) and a pond. The First Parish Unitarian Church and the Second Congregational Church, both draped in a stately white, are located across from each other. The First Parish Meeting House played a prominent role in the film *The Witches of Eastwick*, based on the John Updike novel. Much of the movie was filmed in Cohasset. The 1992 movie *Housesitter*, starring Steve Martin, was also filmed in the town, as were scenes in *The Finest Hours* (along with other areas on the South Shore). Near the common on South Main Street is Cohasset Center Village and its

A re-created town pump depicts life in an earlier time. *Author's photo.*

series of boutiques and a handful of restaurants. The Elisha Doane House, which was constructed about 1750, is now the South Shore Community Center. This lovely three-story white building with black shutters now houses classes and a preschool at 3 North Main Street. The downtown continues onto Depot Court and to Ripley Road, creating an appealing series of specialty shops, gourmet restaurants and utilitarian businesses, mixed in with properties owned by the Cohasset Historical Society. The Historical Society headquarters is at 106 South Main Street in the former library, built in 1903. The society owns and operates two other properties in the center: the Bates Ship Chandlery Museum from 1754, and the 1810 Captain Wilson House, as well as its most recent acquisition, the Beechwood Meeting House, located about a mile from town. In the midst of the downtown are pieces of tangible history, such as the replica of the old town water pump, which sits at the corner of Main and Elm Streets—although it is covered up and not in working condition. Cohasset treasures its history.

Cohasset is unique in many ways. It is part of Norfolk County, while its neighbors belong to Plymouth County. Ever the individualist, Cohasset opted not to join Hull and Hingham under the banner of Plymouth County. The coastal roads and the harbor of Cohasset feel miles away from the town center, although they are geographically close. The same is true with the coast or the center in relation to the Cushing Highway. The sections of the town retain their own feel.

The historic Red Lion Inn is a "mane" attraction in Cohasset. *Author's photo.*

YOUR GUIDE TO HISTORY

Old Town Pump

South Main and Elm Streets, Cohasset, MA 02025

The wooden town pump, which sits covered up at the corner of South Main and Elm Streets, is a re-creation of the water pump that graced this spot in the nineteenth century. This pump and the adjoining slide are made of wood, with a plaque close to the bottom. It was placed there in 1991.

Black Rock House

Once upon a time, the Red Lion Inn was not the only hotel of note in Cohasset. The title was shared with the Black Rock House on Jerusalem Road in the northern part of town. The majestic hotel featured towers, with a central turret providing windswept views of Straits Pond and the Atlantic Ocean. The original inn was built around 1757 by Captain Nathaniel Nichols. It was a modest home. The second incarnation incorporated the former structure and enlarged it substantially. This second version was disassembled, as it blocked nearby cottages' views of the ocean. In 1903, the hotel was rebuilt as the turreted masterpiece seen on old postcards. It met its fate via the wrecking ball in 1968. The inn's history is murky. Some sources say the original structure was built early in the 1700s, but most date it around 1757. Other sources say the original burned, while others speak solely of it being added to. According to some, the final hotel was built in the late nineteenth century, while others pinpoint 1903.

Bates Ship Chandlery Museum

4 Elm Street, Cohasset, MA 02025
781-383-1434, www.cohassethistoricalsociety.org

This building, dating from 1754, was built by Samuel Bates. It is now in the possession of the Cohasset Historical Society. A chandlery was a store to buy equipment and goods to be used on boats. Given the town's seafaring heritage, the chandlery must have been an important place in town. The building moved to its present location in 1957. The museum's collection includes artifacts related to the town's maritime history. Both this building and the Captain John Wilson House, built circa 1810, are owned by the historical society and located at 4 Elm Street, near the intersection with South Main. Wilson was a ship captain, and his former home provides a look into what a Cohasset home of the nineteenth century would have been like, as well as life in the town in the year 1850. It is the last example of an unchanged 1800s home in Cohasset center.

The Red Lion Inn

71 South Main Street, Cohasset, MA
781-383-1704, www.redlioninn1704.com

The history of the Red Lion Inn dates back to 1704, as it was built as the home of Thomas James. In 1772, his grandson Christopher James turned the home into an inn and general store. This building was important in the town's history, as it was used as an infirmary for men who were wrecked at Cohasset's notoriously rocky coast in the *Copenhagen*. Here they were cared for under the guidance of innkeeper Eleazer James. It is hypothesized that this was also a stop on the Underground Railroad. The inn remained in the James family for an amazing 175 years. Today, it thrives as a hotel with a fine restaurant, the Red Lion Tavern. Locals and tourists alike can be found at the inn enjoying a drink. It is a popular destination for weddings and other events.

Atlantic Avenue and Jerusalem Road

Cohasset was a popular summer resort, and the lavish homes on these roads are a testament to this. Although the Black Rock House Hotel is long gone, these exquisitely designed mansions are a mix of the old and the new. The roads that hug the rocky coastline afford sweeping vistas of the Atlantic Ocean and border some of the most prime real estate of the South Shore. Follow Atlantic Avenue (in Hull) from its intersection with Nantasket Avenue. Hull's Atlantic Avenue turns into Forest Avenue in Cohasset; take a quick left onto Jerusalem where it merges into Atlantic Avenue (this time in Cohasset) near Kimball's Point. Follow this road until it meets Margin Street and ends at Cohasset Harbor. This route is highly recommended at any time of the year.

15

NORWELL

"SCITUATE 1636, SOUTH SCITUATE 1849, NORWELL 1888"

Norwell has been able to retain its historic character with the preservation of a vast number of eighteenth and nineteenth century homes. Even driving on Norwell's Main Street, which tends to be busy with traffic, as it connects the seaside town of Scituate to Route 3, one cannot help but be taken aback by the gorgeousness of the residential architecture in this town.

Norwell was originally settled in 1636, but at that time it was part of Satuit, later Scituate. In 1849, it was separated and founded as the town of South Scituate. Thirty-nine years later, the name was changed to Norwell. The overlap here is that in detailing much of the early years of a town such as Norwell, its early history was already included in the chapter on Scituate. Even though Norwell is often thought of in terms of a thriving shipbuilding industry, this was on the decline when it was granted its own status as a town. This being said, it is hard to differentiate where the history of Scituate ends and the story of Norwell begins. Although a piece of Norwell is located on commercial Route 53, the town has retained its historic nature. Popular are the many pieces of protected land that offer miles of hiking trails to the visitor.

The first colonists in this part of Scituate were Cornet Robert Stetson and his wife, Honour Tucker Stetson. They were granted a large swath of land, including what is now known as Stetson Meadows Park. The town-owned Sergeant Samuel Stetson House, built in the late 1600s, is waiting for a new permanent home as of this writing and has been on blocks awaiting relocation. Another important family to Norwell is the Jacob family, later "Jacobs." This

Get lost on the boardwalks of Norwell's Recreation Path. *Author's photo.*

family homestead is located in the Assinippi section. Assinippi straddles the Norwell and Hanover town lines. The name translates to "rocky water." The Jacobs farmhouse and barns are owned by the Town of Norwell. It held Jacobses until 1939, when it was deeded to the group that would become Historic New England. It was later passed into the hands of the town in 1988. It is located at the corner of Jacobs Lane and Main Street near the Jacobs Conservation Area and Jacobs Pond, a popular park with hiking trails. Paths flank the northern and eastern shorelines. The Jacobs Homestead was built around 1726, and it is the headquarters of the Norwell Historical Society. It can be rented out for functions and also is the site of seasonal events such as the spring opening of the farm and Christmas at the farmhouse.

The settlement in this area of Scituate was unique. Scituate's seashore, given its expansive coastline, had little similarity to this area. Agriculture was the main way of life. Eventually, the raising of poultry was popular in town, enough that the town pleaded for a state police barracks to be put here to prevent poultry thieves. This was the basis for the state police barracks still located in the center of Norwell. Norwell's early industry included grist- and sawmills. In 1642, the Second Parish of Scituate, which would be known as the First Parish of Norwell, was established. The church building that still holds this parish community was constructed in 1830. Norwell's earliest residents are buried in its various cemeteries. The Church Hill Cemetery dates from 1728. There is a Celtic cross marking the former site of St. Andrew's Episcopal Church, which existed between 1731 and 1811 in the southern section of town, near the Stetson family property. Stetsons are among the families interred here. The First Parish Cemetery, located near the First Parish Church, dates from 1725. Among the notable burials here are writer John Cheever and Madame Cushing, who was the wife of Chief Justice William Cushing (who is buried in Scituate). A Quaker cemetery and meetinghouse were once present in Norwell, dating from 1661. This was located near the North River at the end of the present Chittenden Lane. Stones at the Second Church Cemetery, which include gravestones harkening back to 1689, represent the oldest markers in the town. River Street was known for its shipbuilders' homes, while Main Street was lined with homes of doctors and ministers.

Norwell is often associated with the shipbuilding industry, which thrived on the North River in the eighteenth and nineteenth centuries. Along with the actual shipyards was the peripheral industry that came with it. The North River marks the border between Hanover and Pembroke and flows to form the boundaries between Norwell and Marshfield and Scituate and

Marshfield. The mouth of the river was altered due to the Portland Gale of 1898, which is why Humarock in Scituate is only accessible via Marshfield. Prior to this, the North and South Rivers' route culminated together before accessing the sea. The *Columbia*, which was the first American ship that sailed around the world, was built on the North River in 1773 at the Briggs' Shipyard at Hobart's Landing. The shipyard was operational from 1687 to 1845 and produced 59 vessels. The *Columbia*, detailed further in the Scituate chapter, was built by James Briggs. It was eighty-three feet in length and weighed 280 tons. One of its most significant voyages was to China, by rounding Cape Horn in South America, and then stopping in Hawaii. The ship also traveled to the northwestern area of the United States. In Oregon, the vessel discovered a major waterway, and it was named the Columbia River. The other shipyards in this area of Scituate included Brooks Tilden, Block House, Chittenden, Curtis-Wanton Yards, Rogers Shipyard, the Fox Hill Yard and Bald Hill/Shipyard. The last large boat that was built at a North River shipyard was constructed at Chittenden Shipyard in 1871. This was the *Helen M. Foster*. (A smaller boat was built and launched at this river in the 1990s.) All in all, 1,025 watercraft were constructed on the North River. The greatest number to be built in one year was 30 in 1801.

South Scituate desired to separate from the town of Scituate and eventually did so in 1849. This was in part due to a financial dispute. The federal government granted each state a certain allotment of funds due to a surplus. The state then divided the money by the town's population. The residents of the southern section of Scituate were unhappy about how the Town of Scituate (which was located close to the ocean) handled this task. Scituate lent money to residents. The folks of South Scituate opposed this. This, coupled with the fact that Scituate identified itself with its ties to the ocean, caused the southern section to desire independence. Norwell's history is congruent not only with Scituate but also other towns on the North River such as Marshfield and Pembroke. In the twenty-first century, Norwell is primarily residential. It is a wealthy town, with large, rambling, impeccably restored old farmhouses or modern mansions. Norwell has pride in its school system and its recreational activities. The biggest commercial district is on Washington Street, Route 53, with restaurants and stores. The center of Norwell also has a small shopping area with restaurants and other businesses. Norwell also has a vast collection of conservation land. Among its popular family-friendly places in town are Hornstra Farms and the South Shore Natural Science Center, which is also the location of the farmers' market. The latter's address is 48 Jacobs Lane.

YOUR GUIDE TO HISTORY

Albert F. Norris Reservation

10 Dover Street, Norwell, MA 02061
http://www.thetrustees.org/places-to-visit/south-of-boston/norris-reservation.html

Among Norwell's beautiful collection of green spaces is the Norris Reservation. The trustees operate this property at 10 Dover Street, near the center of town. Included here are a former millpond and a boardwalk that traverses wetlands, with views along the North River. Look for the old boathouse that is part of the reservation. This preserve was the property of Albert and Eleanor Norris, and after Albert's death, Eleanor left the property to the trustees to thwart developers from claiming pieces of the 99-acre parcel (today it is 129 acres in all). Her one action helped preserve a natural piece of the South Shore for posterity. Thank you, Eleanor. The parking lot is off Dover Street near the center of town.

For a true agrarian experience, make sure to stop at Hornstra Farms. *Author's photo.*

Hornstra Farms

246 Prospect Street, Norwell, MA 02061
781-749-1222, www.hornstrafarms.com

Hornstra is much more than a run-of-the-mill farm store. It is known for its milk, which is still delivered by truck. The cows at Hornstra are viewable from either inside the barn or outside, depending on their location. Calves seem to always be in the lower level of the barn, accessible from the side of the main driveway. Kids get a kick out of seeing the young cows up close and personal. The farm store is small but contains locally sourced and seasonal items. Hornstra is known for its ice cream made on site. The creamery offers ice cream cones at the window (in season) and in cartons to go. The Hornstras started their dairy farm in Hingham in 1915, after moving to the United States from Holland three years earlier. In 2009, the fourth generation of Hornstras, John and his wife, Lauren, bought this property, which was known as the Loring Farm. After years of rehabilitation and renovation, the farm store opened in 2014, with milk bottled from here a year earlier. Dairy farms were once a common sight on the South Shore; Hornstra is one of the last of its kind. Sign up for fresh milk delivered to your home.

16

ROCKLAND

"HATHERLY GRANT 1656, ABINGTON 1712, TOWN OF ROCKLAND INC. A.D. 1874"

This historical background of Rockland is much different than that of most towns on the South Shore. For one, it is not situated on the ocean; for another, its past is rooted in the manufacturing heyday of the nineteenth century. Where many of the interior towns on the South Shore had industry but were primarily agrarian in nature, Rockland's industrial heritage sets it apart. This is similar to Whitman and Abington. These three towns all made up the original town of Abington, with Whitman, incorporated in 1875, being named eleven years later in 1886. Rockland, although incorporated as part of the town of Abington in 1673 and known as East Abington, became its own town in 1873. With its relatively short history as compared to other towns in the region, the industrial and post-industrial periods are covered here, with earlier information provided in the Abington chapter.

The land that became Rockland was part of the original nine-mile square known as the Conihasset Grant, an extension of the Hatherly Grant, in 1656. The Hatherly Grant was a parcel of land granted to Timothy Hatherly and other settlers of Scituate in 1633. Although Rockland's history is closely linked to its manufacturing industry, the heavily wooded land was originally used for lumber in the shipyards of the North River. Once the land was left mostly barren due to the deforestation of the trees for lumber, farming took over. In 1712, Abington was incorporated. As in many neighboring towns, shoe manufacturing would define Rockland. The first shoe shop was opened

The sun is overhead at the Emerson Shoe Lofts, a former shoe factory that has been converted into loft-style apartments. *Jaclyn Lamothe.*

in 1793 by Thomas Hunt. It quickly grew. By 1832, there were six factories in East Abington, and more shoes were produced here than in Brockton. By 1865, East Abington shoe factories were employing three thousand people generating $3.5 million in income. The split between East Abington and Abington started to form in 1874 over money. This led to East Abington striking out on its own as Rockland a year later.

Today, Rockland is known more for its geographic location than what is found inside the town. With its proximity to the seaside towns such as Hingham, Scituate and Cohasset, but with more affordable real estate tags, it has become a great choice for families who are looking for a quiet town that is close to the action of the South Shore. Its accessibility to Route 3 (which passes through the town) puts Boston at under a half hour's drive (given average traffic) and is also less than an hour's drive to Cape Cod. Although proximity may be important to the prospective home buyer or the Boston commuter, this chapter focuses on what Rockland itself has to offer, historically and in the present day. For a glimpse of Rockland's past, it is best to start on Union Street. In what is known as the Lower Union Historic District, magnificent mansions (many of which were built in the 1800s) line both sides of the road. The wide boulevard that is Union Street is the main road of Rockland. The Union Street neighborhood was known as "The Hill." The road, without curvature, is lined with stately homes, municipal buildings—including the library and former high school—and storefronts. Rockland forgoes the typical New England heritage of town squares and winding streets found in other villages of the South Shore. Although some buildings have survived the ravages of time, former magnificent structures, such as the Rockland Savings Bank, have been lost. Much of the town has a suburban feel today; it is most walkable in the center of town, down Union Street.

In the twenty-first century, many of Rockland's former factories—which, by the way, are unusual in that they are made of wood and not the traditional brick—are now repurposed for use as artists' studios. The studios are private, but a few times a year, the public is invited to view the collections, which are typically available for purchase. Popular recreational spots include the Rail Trail, which was once a rail spur, part of the Old Colony Railroad and the Rockland Town Forest.

One neat feature that has recently been in the town spotlight is the Tramp House located at 198 Spring Street. It looks like a small shack. The building dates from 1876 and was used as a temporary boardinghouse for vagabonds. There were five such structures in Massachusetts, including another on the South Shore in Kingston, but it is on private property today. These were often located near railroad tracks, as those riding the rails from town to town had a lack of permanent housing. For years, the Tramp House sat in a state of disrepair and was even used by the Little League as a storage shed. It has been reclaimed by the historical commission. What is now North River Collaborative School was once the almshouse and situated right next to the Tramp House. It was used heavily, as in 1900 alone, 564 wanderers stayed there. Today, the house is undergoing a process of restoration.

YOUR GUIDE TO HISTORY

Repurposed Factories

The E.T. Wright Building, the sandpaper factory and Emerson Shoe Lofts
Rockland, MA 02070

Now repurposed, the E.T. Wright shoe factory and the sandpaper factory are presently used as artist studios. Another former factory, the Emerson

Typical grand architecture of Union Street. *Author's photo.*

Shoe factory, later known as the Codman Building, has been converted into loft-style apartments.

The E.T. Wright Building was the home of Just Wright Shoes, a widely popular shoe brand named for its owner, Elwin T. Wright. The wooden factory once had a tower adorning it. By 1912, it employed seven hundred people churning out three thousand pairs of shoes a day. The factory now showcases the work of a South Shore artist collective known as the 4th Floor Artists. Gallery 4 is an exhibition space on the first floor of the Wright building and displays works of its resident artists. Visit www.4thfloorartists.com for more information. The E.T. Wright Building is located at 379 Liberty Street in Rockland, and the sandpaper factory is at 83 East Water Street.

Although these are two former factories that are semi-open to the public, many additional shoe factories put Rockland on the industrial map. In addition to the Emerson Shoe Factory, with its loft-style apartments, located at 51 Maple Street and online at www.emersonshoelofts.com, another shoe factory, the J.E. French Company, was also located in Rockland. The Rice and Hutchins factory was one of the largest, built in 1865, and was located on Water Street. The Hurley Brothers opened the Hurley shoe factory on Church Street. From all of the shoes made in town, Rockland's downtown on Union Street was a hotbed of shopping, and of course, shoe stores were abundant. Rockland and environs counted for 27 percent of the nation's shoe manufacturers.

Rockland Rail Trail

Rockland, MA 02360

The rail trail traverses the town from east to west following the former route of the Hanover branch of the Old Colony Railroad. The 2.6-mile rail trail connects Rockland with Abington and Hanover. Currently, the eastern terminus extends into Abington at the corner of Monroe and Birch Streets. Most of the trail is hard-packed dirt with some parts paved and with crushed stone; it's good for biking, walking and running. A nonprofit group rehabilitated the old rail line into a path for the public to enjoy. Access it from different places in town, but two popular parking lots are the one at the corner of East Water and Union Streets next to the Dunkin' and the Banner bar/restaurant as well as parking at either Rockland High School or Memorial Park Elementary School.

Rockland's rail trail, perfect for a stroll in any weather. *Author's photo.*

17

WHITMAN

"BIRTHPLACE OF THE CHOCOLATE CHIP COOKIE"

The town of Whitman has undergone many incarnations and name changes since its inception as part of the Bridgewater Purchase of 1649. The deed of the Bridgewater Purchase was brokered between Massasoit and Myles Standish, Samuel Nash and Constant Southworth, all of Duxbury. Bridgewater, in the hands of the English, was originally part of Duxbury. Even before that, the land later to become Whitman was known to the Native Americans who inhabited this region as Manamooskeagin or "great green place of shaking grass." This land, along with the area of the future towns of Rockland and Abington, was collectively referred to as "Old Abington," as both Whitman and Rockland were named South Abington and East Abington, respectively. As part of Bridgewater, the region of Whitman was known as Little Comfort. It was not until 1875 that it received township status as South Abington. The modern name Whitman, adopted in 1886, honors local gentleman Augustus Whitman and his family.

Although agriculture was a primary way of life, industry would define the town of Whitman. At one time, dairy farms were prevalent in Whitman. Today, only the farm at Peaceful Meadows (which makes superb ice cream) remains. Peaceful Meadows is located at 98 North Bedford Street (Route 18). The first mill deed was awarded in 1693 on the Schumatuscacant River, which is named for the once present beaver. Coming from

First Congregational Church in Whitman has greeted worshippers since 1807. *Author's photo.*

Abington, the river winds close to the center of town. Industry expanded exponentially through the eighteenth century into the nineteenth century with booming manufacturing of such products as shoes, cannonballs, nails and tacks. Whitman resident Colonel Aaron Hobart supplied the timber for the USS *Constitution*. The shoe industry (along with chocolate chip cookies) put Whitman on the map with around twenty shoemakers. The Commonwealth Shoe and Leather Company, a highly successful business, made the ever-popular Bostonian shoe. Although production ceased in the 1970s, the former factory has been beautifully restored into loft-style apartments at 7 Marble Street. The Bostonian shoe is still manufactured today, but production is not located in Whitman. The circa 1864 Dunbar, Hobart and Whidden Tack Factory was at one time the largest factory of its kind in the world. Another tack and nail factory, DB Gurney Nail and Tack, began in 1825 and is still headquartered in town, making nails and tacks to this day.

Whitman boys served their country in its nation's wars, including the American Revolution and the Civil War. One individual, Benjamin Gardner Jr., even participated in the Boston Tea Party. In addition to shoemaking, Whitman is best known for being the birthplace of the chocolate chip cookie. A recipe invented by Ruth Graves Wakefield dates from 1938. She served the piping-hot cookies accented with Nestlé semisweet chocolate pieces that she broke up with an ice pick at the Toll House Inn, built circa 1817. Unfortunately, the inn was destroyed by fire on New Year's Eve 1984. A commemorative sign stands at the location of the former restaurant at 362 Bedford Street (Route 18). Since Whitman was a town based on industry, some former mill sites can still be seen today; others have been completely destroyed. While rehabilitation has breathed a second life into certain factories, others lay in ruin with their fate in question.

Whitman retains its small factory town feel, with a mid-twentieth rather than a twenty-first-century ambiance. The walkable downtown is self-sufficient, containing restaurants, stores and coffee shops. The town common is a serene place for a stroll and features a pond with a fountain. However, Whitman has more than meets the eye. The past has been reshaped in the form of rehabilitated factories, and the foundation of a roundhouse remains on its former Old Colony railroad line.

The Bostonian Shoe Lofts, another former shoe factory that has been converted into loft-style apartments. *Author's photo.*

YOUR GUIDE TO HISTORY

Toll House Inn Marker

362 Bedford Street, Whitman, MA 02382

On busy Route 18, also known as Bedford Street, note the sign and commemorative plaque at number 362 marking the dedication of the Toll House Inn and cookie. In 1938, this site saw the birth of the chocolate chip cookie or, as inventor/baker Ruth Graves Wakefield originally called it, the "Toll House Crunch Cookie." The Wakefields bought the inn in 1930 and named it the Toll House Inn. The sign read "1709," creating fictitious lore of the building's date of origin, since the building's construction was finished in 1817. The name Toll House Inn has been disputed too. Some sources say there was a toll to be paid here by travelers en route to Boston or New Bedford, but others insist the name and 1709 date were a fabricated or embellished past of the building concocted by the owners. Either way, the Wakefields' restaurant was known for its seafood dishes and desserts, including, most emphatically, Ruth's cookie, loaded with those scrumptious chunks of semisweet chocolate. Ruth's name will always be synonymous with the iconic chocolate chip cookie. The sign and plaque can be seen between a Wendy's restaurant and a Walgreens drugstore.

Former Roundhouse Park

Adjacent to Whitman MBTA commuter rail station at 383 South Avenue, Whitman, MA 02382

The Old Colony Railroad ran through Whitman from the years 1847 to 1959. (The Whitman to East Bridgewater spur ended in 1925, with the tracks taken up in 1940.) When commuter service to Boston expanded, many of these old lines found new life. The Whitman Station reopened in 1997 and is part of the Kingston-Plymouth commuter rail line. During the

The former roundhouse site in Whitman is now a little-known park. *Jaclyn Lamothe.*

excavation, workers uncovered the foundation of a former roundhouse, a circular building that was used for servicing the trains. This has been dedicated as a park and can be seen by commuter rail passengers from the train window. The outline of the roundhouse can be viewed, as well as railroad tracks shooting off from the former building site. There are historical markers there too. Due to all of the industry, Whitman was heavily trafficked by trains and even included two train depots in town. In 2014, a local teenager spruced up the park for his Eagle Scout project.

18

IN THE FOOTSTEPS
OF THE FOREFATHERS

PLYMOUTH, MARSHFIELD, DUXBURY, HALIFAX, KINGSTON

Names of or references to the earliest settlers can be seen everywhere you look in the South Shore, from Myles Standish State Park and the town of Carver to any business bearing the word *Pilgrim* in its title and streets with monikers of Bradford, Howland and Brewster. As a historical guide, this book has the distinction of being able to focus on the earliest days of colonial America. Plymouth Colony, along with Jamestown, was one of the first British settlements in North America. While the Plymouth chapter of the book focuses on the Separatists' journey, this chapter depicts the spread of the forefathers as they left the confines of their original settlement. Sections of this chapter showcase actual buildings or artifacts from the first colonists, whereas others list monuments and memorials to them erected at much later dates. The rest, such as the Winslow House in Marshfield, were not actual homes of *Mayflower* passengers but were inhabited by a long line of direct descendants. Please note, many, many forefather sites are located in Plymouth. For a fantastic collection of artifacts related to them, visit Pilgrim Hall Museum in Plymouth.

The impressive National Monument to the Forefathers is an often-overlooked gem in Plymouth. *Adam Mannar.*

National Monument to the Forefathers

Allerton Street, Plymouth, MA 02360

Rising out of the hills of Plymouth, this colossus will be one of the most impressive statues you will view in your lifetime. Unlike most attractions in Plymouth, which are both well marked and/or on a main road, this monument stands proudly by itself on Allerton Street—you can't miss it. The National Monument to the Forefathers was completed in 1889 in commemoration of the Pilgrims' plight. Faith is the centerpiece of the eighty-one-foot granite statue as she points heavenward. Seated around the base of the monument at her feet are the figures of Education, Law, Liberty and Morality, all in human representations. Even smaller statuary are engraved in the seated figures' benches. At the base of the seated statues are reliefs. Each of the statuary's names represents a value of America, all of which harken back to the days of the forefathers. The statue's sheer immensity is startling, as is the fact that many residents of Plymouth are not even familiar with it. For a journey detailing the lives of the forefathers, this statue is a great place to start. Although it was built almost 270 years after their arrival, it reflects how the determination and values of the Pilgrims have been ingrained in the essence of America.

Myles Standish Monument

Crescent Street, Duxbury, MA 02332

Looking north from Plymouth Bay, a large granite tower with a figure perched atop rises above the tree line at 116 feet. Located on a hillside of Standish's estate is a stone tribute to the military leader of the Plymouth Colony. Standish, who arrived on the *Mayflower* with the Pilgrims, led the group through the tempestuous early years. After the obligatory tenure of the group settling near their point of origin, Standish, along with others, including John Alden and William Brewster, took to the north of the original settlement in what is known today as Duxbury. The cornerstone was laid in 1872 to much fanfare before a crowd of ten thousand. The tower was not finished until 1898 due to funding issues, leaving the tower partially constructed for a time. Upon close investigation, the granite is different colors. During the era in which the tower was built, Standish, along with other of his Pilgrim brethren, were touted as heroes and a part of American mythology. He was also popularized in *The Courtship of Miles Standish* by Henry Wadsworth Longfellow.

The tower is capped with a fourteen-foot granite figure of Standish. He has one arm outstretched, with the other holding a copy of the Plymouth Colony charter under his arm. Standish's garb is typical of other depictions of him.

The tower and surrounding park are located off Crescent Street in Duxbury. If the gates are closed, park near them and walk up. During certain weekends, the gates are open with direct access to the tower. When this is the case, there is a better chance that the actual tower is available to walk up. The hike is 125 steps, or nine stories. The stone tubular tower is stark inside, with a series of windows providing the only light. The walk up a spiral metal staircase with a series of informational pamphlets ends with a tight 360-degree viewshed. There are windows that overlook the bay and countryside in each direction. Duxbury and Plymouth Bay can be seen, and on a clear day, the view extends all the way over to Blue Hills.

The Legs of Myles Standish

20 Dwight Street, Halifax, MA 02338

The monument of Myles Standish in Duxbury is capped with a fourteen-foot statue of the leader. The actual figure's history has been ill fated. Although the statue was completed in 1898, twenty years later, it was already in a state of disrepair. In 1920, the statue was placed under the jurisdiction of the State of Massachusetts. (Currently, it is operated by the Massachusetts Department of Conservation and Recreation.) Two years later, on August 26, 1922, the Standish figure was struck by lightning, decapitating him and dismembering one of his arms. In the mid-1920s, he stood high atop the tower with arm outstretched—albeit headless—gazing east toward Duxbury Bay. In 1926, a new head and other body features were ready to be placed on top of the remaining body. The remaining legs could not hold the weight of the newly designed head, so the original legs had to be scrapped. In 1930, Myles was reconstructed—except for his right arm and his chest, which were original.

This gets to the odd occurrence of a set of Myles Standish's legs displayed on a backroad in a neighborhood in Halifax. Dwight Street is a small road

The legs of Myles Standish are tucked away on a side street in Halifax. *Author's photo.*

in the Monponsett section of Halifax just over the Hanson border close to the twin lakes of Monponsett Pond. The bottom half of Standish was found in a quarry in Quincy where it was disposed of once the new legs were created. The twelve-foot legs include an unopened time capsule between his feet. The display at 20 Dwight Street sits atop a manufactured railroad bed and next to an old barrel factory with a plaque describing Monponsett on it. The trip that the legs took between Quincy and Halifax was provided by a police escort. The local residents of Halifax who lobbied for this were happy to bring Myles back since he owned a large tract of land in present-day Halifax, along with his Duxbury estate and farm.

Myles Standish Cemetery and Gravesite

Chestnut Street, Duxbury, MA 02332

Notable individuals interred at the oldest maintained cemetery in the United States include Myles Standish and John and Priscilla Alden. The burial ground is on the site of the first meetinghouse in Duxbury. It is well preserved, although this was not always the case. Many of the monuments were placed long after the burials. Although the cemetery is well manicured today, for much of the nineteenth century it was an overgrown field that cattle would use for grazing. The earliest markers were destroyed by the elements. The first carved stone is that of Captain Jonathan Alden, which dates from 1697.

Many of the stones are from the eighteenth century, although many more bodies are buried here than are markers present. Myles Standish's body was exhumed for the first time in the late nineteenth century at the location hypothesized to be the family plot. A more fitting monument was erected in his tribute. It is an imposing structure befitting the Pilgrims' military leader; it is flanked on all sides by cannons. The cemetery contains early American gravestone art, including the ominous death's head. It is located on the north side of Chestnut Street surrounded by a fence. At first glance, it is hard to see that it is a burial ground from the street since the stones are scattered and mostly located in the left-hand side of the cemetery.

Alden House Historic Site

105 Alden Street, Duxbury, MA 02332
781-934-9092, www.alden.org, Admission $8

John and Priscilla (Mullins) Alden were *Mayflower* passengers. The Aldens married in 1621. John was a cooper (barrel maker) who was not a Pilgrim, but he went on to take a prominent role within the Plymouth Colony. The poem *The Courtship of Miles Standish* speaks of a love triangle between Priscilla, John and Myles. It is not clear if there was any truth to this or if it was the product of oral tradition. The poem and the year of John Alden's death are not the only controversial issues surrounding the Aldens. The home, which houses a museum today, has two separate dates of origin. Most scholars say that it was erected in 1700, but others believe it was from an earlier date, 1653. Either way, the house is one of the oldest in Massachusetts.

John and Priscilla Alden moved out of Plymouth in 1628 and settled on one hundred acres of land in Duxbury. The location of their original home is close to this site. It is accessible via a path from the homesite, marked by a boulder close to sports fields. The Alden land has been passed down from the original owners and has been operated by the family in the form of the Alden Kindred Foundation since 1907. The original hundred acres include the land that the nearby Art Complex Museum is situated on. The house is furnished with period pieces, and the museum is available for tours from June to October, Wednesday through Saturday. Visitors are allowed to walk around the grounds year-round.

Winslow House

634 Careswell Street, Marshfield, MA 02050
781-837-5753, www.winslowhouse.org, Admission $5

The Winslow House in Marshfield sits on land that once belonged to *Mayflower* passenger Governor Edward Winslow. The home was built by his grandson Isaac Winslow, a prominent judge and councilman, in 1699. The house was nicknamed Careswell, which was derived from Kerswell, the name of the Winslow family estate in England. The Winslows remained an important family in Marshfield, and the home passed from one generation to the next until it was acquired by Daniel Webster in 1822. Webster never lived at the home, but it was part of his larger estate, used for various purposes. His law office, full of Webster memorabilia, is located adjacent to the Winslow House and is also a museum today. After it was sold to Webster, the property passed through several families. It was eventually acquired by the Winslow Associates, a group that still runs the home today under the banner of the Winslow House Association.

Jabez Howland House

33 Sandwich Street, Plymouth, MA 02360
www.pilgrimjohnhowlandsociety.org/The_Jabez_Howland_House, Admission $6

The Jabez Howland House, circa 1667, is the only home still standing in Plymouth that was inhabited by a Pilgrim who arrived on the *Mayflower*. John Howland and his wife, Elizabeth Tilley Howland, spent their winters in this home. After John died in the early 1670s, his wife and son, Jabez, lived in the home until 1680, when Jabez sold it. It was a private home until 1912, when it was turned into a museum. The home is full of period furnishings and includes artifacts from the primary Howland homesite at Rocky Nook in Kingston. The collection also includes correspondence from President Franklin Delano Roosevelt, who was a descendant of Howland. Letters from Winston Churchill, who was considered a cousin of the Howlands since he was a descendant of John's brother Arthur, are also here. Fun fact: another of Howland's brothers, Henry, was an ancestor of Presidents Gerald Ford and Richard Nixon. The museum is open seven days a week from 10:00 a.m. to 4:30 p.m. from Memorial Day to October.

John Howland Homesite

67 Howlands Lane, Kingston, MA 02364
www.pilgrimjohnhowlandsociety.org

Upon arrival in Plymouth, John Howland lived in town until the mid-1630s, when he built a farm in Duxbury. From here, he purchased a parcel of land to build a home at Rocky Nook in what is now Kingston in 1638. He sold the Duxbury farm in 1640 and lived in Rocky Nook until his death around the year 1673. (He wintered in Plymouth at the foot of Watson's Hill, now called the Jabez Howland House.) Although the Kingston home no longer stands, the site has been preserved as a monument since 1921. The archaeological pieces displayed at the Jabez Howland House have been culled from here. The preservation land includes an inscribed boulder and a kiosk along with a marker for the homesite.

19

THE ANNUAL HERRING RUN

SOUTH SHORE WIDE

Nothing rings in spring on the South Shore like the arrival of the river herring to the region's waterways. These anadromous fish swim upstream from the ocean to their freshwater destinations to spawn each spring after spending their lives in the ocean. The natural life cycle of the river herring, specifically blueback and alewife, was severely hampered by the damming of rivers and waterways. In recent years, there has been a strong conservation effort to return the fish to their original behavior. With the un-damming of rivers, fish have been able to repopulate their habitats. These efforts have been underway throughout New England, especially in many former industrial areas, which often harnessed the water for power. From Maine to Connecticut, the work of government and conservation groups has increased these freshwater-spawning fish. In the South Shore, the river herring are the primary beneficiaries of the access to their spawning sites. From Florida to the Canadian Maritime Provinces, the population of much of the Eastern Seaboard's river herring has decreased due to industrialization, as well as overfishing, streamflow depletion from water withdrawals and pollution. More locally, river herring run through the Nemasket River in Middleborough. Sites on Cape Cod and the islands are also popular viewing spots for the fish's trip from ocean to fresh water. River herring are an essential food source for birds and larger fish. Since river herring populations are at historic lows and are being restored, it is illegal to catch them. Herring are

The Plimoth Grist Mill has a fish ladder alongside it to help herring on their journey. *Author's photo.*

not typically eaten as food by humans these days; instead, they are utilized as bait for larger fish.

Herring are born in fresh water, and then, during the summer or autumn months, they swim to the ocean to live. They spend their lives, which can be up to twelve years or so, at sea. They return to their place of origin to procreate when they are three or four years old, or sexually mature. Many herring die during their journey, be it from predators, pollution or the strenuousness of their trip. An average alewife's length is between eight and a half and thirteen inches long, weighing between eight and nine ounces. Although river herring runs are present in most towns on the South Shore, three major routes are highlighted here. Plymouth's Town Brook is the route the herring travel from the ocean to Billington Sea. In Pembroke, the appropriately named Herring Brook is the site of their route, and in Weymouth, the Back River is the path they take. These three different herring runs showcase three diverse geographic locations of the South Shore: Weymouth in the north, Pembroke in the middle and Plymouth in the south. Additionally, many other towns include mechanisms such as fish ladders, which are used to help passage, though these are a compromise that requires much human intervention to work and not as effective as dam removal for restoration. This includes Veteran's Memorial Park's fish ladder in Marshfield on the South River and the Old Oaken Bucket fish ladder at the First Herring Brook in Scituate. The English settlers of the South Shore knew the importance of the fish. Much controversy arose as water sources used by the fish were blocked. As early as 1817, the Massachusetts legislature made it mandatory that dam owners in the town of Braintree provide a passageway for the herring. At the end of April and early May, these waterways, filled with the silver fish, are quite the spectacle. After a typical gloomy New England winter, the arrival of the river herring welcomes spring.

PLYMOUTH

For the Wampanoag and the Pilgrim settlers, river herring was a major source of their diet. The protein-rich food was also used to fertilize their soil, a tactic the Englishmen learned from the Indigenous population. Historically, the fish were often eaten smoked or salted. Given their bony nature, they were not the tastiest. The first written account of river herring in the new land was from Charles Whitborne in the 1616 publication of *The True Travels of John Smith*. His quote references the plentiful quantity of the fish. The small

A fish ladder in Hanson. *Author's photo*.

fish were essential to the existence and survival of the Plymouth Colony. The herring populated the Town Brook, the site of the freshwater source that enabled the Pilgrims to settle there. Before industrialization and damming of the brook, the quantity of river herring populating the brook was roughly 1 million. The number was cut drastically to around 150,000 fish in the first years of the twenty-first century.

Spawning river herring were rounded up by the staff of the Massachusetts Department of Marine Fisheries and taken to a freshwater location so that they could spawn uninhibited or unobstructed. The brook, once dammed to be used for water power, no longer served an industrial purpose in the 2000s. There were a total of six obstructions on the brook, but dams were methodically dismantled to allow the passage of the fish. At the Plimoth Grist Mill, a fish ladder lets them swim up from the lower part of Town Brook into the upper through a tunnel. With the work done to restore their natural cycle, the herring population in the brook has increased. The culminating achievement for the fish is their arrival at Billington Sea, a freshwater pond accessible from Morton Park in Plymouth. Volunteers count the fish and are available to answer any questions during the springtime river herring run. In

2016, 199,368 river herring were counted. Plymouth holds an annual Herring Run Festival on a Saturday in late April. In addition to information about the natural event, there are diversions for the whole family, including nature walks, talks about the herring and face painting for the kids. In the Plimoth Grist Mill, there are educational river herring related activities as well.

PEMBROKE

The best place to watch the river herring run in Pembroke is at the appropriately named Herring Run Historical Park on the aptly named Herring Brook. (The official name is the Thomas Reading Memorial Herring Run Park.) Unlike Plymouth, which is a waterfront town, Pembroke is landlocked. It does have a number of rivers, brooks, streams and ponds within the confines of the town. This means the fish have quite a journey to make (sixteen miles) from the Atlantic Ocean to the freshwater ponds of Furnace and Oldham in Pembroke. A fishway connects these two ponds—it can be seen underneath Route 14 (Mattakeesett Street). It is easiest to park at either John's Barbershop or Lindy's General Store to walk to see the fishway. The fish's journey begins at the Marshfield-Scituate line, where the North River meets the sea. It travels through the towns of Norwell and Hanover before reaching Pembroke. The North River headwaters are a combination of the Indian Head River and Herring Brook. The Indian Head River branches out through Hanover, and its headwaters are the Indian Head Brook and Drinkwater River. Wampatuck and Maquan Ponds in Hanson are the headwater ponds to the Indian Head Brook. These rivers and brooks were dammed to harness the water for industry starting in colonial times. From 1694 to 1920, dams were built along these waterways, limiting the mobility of the fish. Fish ladders can be seen on West Elm Street at the site of the former Clapp Rubber Factory, which is now Luddam's Ford Park on the Hanover/Pembroke line. The mills on the waterways were forced to keep their gates open during the running of the herring starting in 1742. Herring Run Park is a worthwhile exploration. The Herring Brook travels through it, and it splits near the entrance to the park. Two branches run through the park. Wooden and stone bridges span the waterways. The stone overpass is next to the site of the former waterwheel. Traces of the park's former industrial use remain on the property. The series of brooks and bridges lend to its appeal. Toward the back of the park is a brick grill and picnic tables. Additionally, look for the large oval-shaped boulder. In late April or early

May, there is an annual Fish Fry here, and the event features food, duck races on the brook and child-oriented activities.

In addition to the Herring Run Historical Park, which is located on Route 14 (Barker Street) in Pembroke, there are other conservation lands that allow public access to the brooks where one can see the fish's upstream expedition. The Wildland Trust's Willow Brook Farm Preserve's waterways (Route 14, Barker Street, close to the Herring Run Park) meander through the protected land. Wildlife is abundant; river otters and beaver have even been spotted. Misty Meadows Conservation Land (the trailhead is at 34 Ingham Way) also has access to the North River. Do not be confused when turning onto Misty Meadow Road off Route 53 because it looks like a housing development. It is just that, with a granite marker indicating the entrance between two houses. Parking is on the street, but as of 2019, the conservation land access is not well marked.

Unlike other groomed riversides, the Pembroke rivers and brooks do not have miles of walkable trails alongside them, and the rivers are only accessible in certain spots. Fish were such an important source of sustainability in these parts that the Indigenous name for this region was Nemassakeesett or "place of much fish." Shad seldom make an appearance, but have been seen in Herring Brook. By the late 1990s, Pembroke's rivers and streams were almost depleted of their natural inhabitants. Through conservation efforts and the deconstruction of infrastructure (although there is more to go), the numbers of fish have increased, although the millions of fish that swam upstream during the early 1600s are still certainly not within sight. In 2016, the herring count numbered 300,000. In comparison to Plymouth, whose herring run has become a bit of a tourist attraction and is located in a highly populated section of town, Pembroke's is much less publicized but still offers visitors a rewarding trip to witness the steady struggle as the fish return from their ocean home to spawn in freshwater sources.

WEYMOUTH

In contrast to Plymouth's herring run, much of which is naturally scenic, and Pembroke's, which is a mixture of rural and suburban, Weymouth's starts along protected natural areas but also winds its way through populated neighborhoods and under state roads. The spawning route of the river herring here travels from the ocean at Hingham Bay and up Weymouth's Back River. The entrance to the tidal river is surrounded by Abigail Adams and Esker Point Parks in Weymouth and Stodder's Neck and Bare Cove in Hingham. The river forms the natural boundary between these towns. It is marshy, wide and serene here before it narrows as the Herring Brook, and the fish swim through the populated neighborhoods of East Weymouth. The journey is relatively short in comparison to that of the Pembroke fish, as their freshwater spawning grounds is Whitman's Pond, which has public access off of Middle Street. This is at the site of the Herring Run Pool Park at the corner of Commercial and Water Streets. This intersection is the prime location for Weymouth herring watching during their annual run. The river route is 4.8 miles from the harbor to Whitman's Pond and has six fish ladders along the way. Between Jackson Square and Whitman's Pond, the herring run travels past Iron Hill Park on Iron Hill Street. The park and street were named for the bog iron harvested from Whitman's Pond. Occurring naturally, it was used in the Weymouth Iron Works, at one time the largest employer in Weymouth. Originally, the herring continued their freshwater journey past Whitman's Pond and into the Mill and Swamp Rivers, eventually ending at Weymouth Great Pond, which is used today as the primary source of town drinking water. Although the Weymouth alewives' journey is relatively short at under 5 miles, with the six fish ladders, including one that is 72 feet in length with 117 steps—it is an arduous one. The Weymouth route is the second-most-populated herring run in Massachusetts. The earliest recorded incidence of the fish dates from 1648. As in other areas, the fish population declined with industrialization and pollution, but through conservation efforts, it is back on the rise.

All three of these diverse river herring runs showcase the plight of this relatively small anadromous fish. Each path travels through different terrain, but the fish have one goal in mind, the freshwater spawning rivers and pond. The focus is usually on the mature fish swimming upriver to spawn from salt to fresh water, but the diametric opposite occurs as the fry, or baby fish, begin at the pond and follow the brooks and streams as they flow, traveling downstream to the ocean. While much focus in restoring these fish has been on their upstream migration, this downstream migration is equally challenged by human disruption, largely due to the overuse of water during the summertime, leaving the young fish high and dry. Herring, which were an important part of the region's sustainability as a food source for both European and Indigenous peoples alike, were nearly wiped out due to man-made disruption of natural habitats and life cycles. Fortunately, awareness and conservation efforts continue to grow, which will result in more and more fish being spotted swimming upstream each spring. Not only do the herring welcome springtime, but they also are a tangible piece of history that naturally occurs in the present just as in the past.

20

FORMER MILITARY HOLDINGS

SOUTH SHORE WIDE

When visiting beachside resorts with majestic ocean views or quaint colonial villages, it is not obvious that the South Shore was once full of sites dedicated to our nation's defense. From Fort Revere in Hull, a former army stronghold that became operational in the Revolutionary War years, to the shipyard in Hingham, where destroyers were manufactured, the South Shore's sites are many and varied, credited with greatly helping the war effort. Some are hidden but accessible to the public, such as the former barracks at Wompatuck State Park or at Union Point, the former naval base that has now been developed into a self-sufficient community. Lookout towers in Marshfield, Plymouth and Scituate gave watch over the sea, while the battleship the USS *Salem* is docked at the Quincy Harbor and is visitable today.

WOMPATUCK STATE PARK

204 Union Street, Hingham, MA 02043
www.mass.gov/locations/wompatuck-state-park

Hingham, with its immaculately preserved homes from a bygone era lining Main Street, Central Street and the town center, seems worlds away from nuclear ammunition, bunkers and machine gun shells. The picture-perfect

This jet gives clues to the former use of the property that once was home to the Naval Air Station South Weymouth. *Author's photo.*

community has much green space, a good amount of which was once under the jurisdiction of the U.S. military. Wompatuck State Park, whose entrance is at 204 Union Street in Hingham, is named for Chief Josiah Wampatuck (sometimes spelled Wompatuck), who sold the land to the English in 1655. A chief in the Mattakeesett of the Massachusetts tribe, Wampatuck also deeded the land on which Boston would be built to English settlers. The park is actually located in four towns: Hingham, Cohasset, Scituate and Norwell. Today, it is a popular place to ride bikes, camp, stroll, boat and run. It even has a natural spring, the Mount Blue Spring; visitors can fill up reusable water bottles from this clean water source. Even without knowing the history of Wompatuck, when visitors walk through its many paths and roads, something seems amiss. Be it random fire hydrants, power lines or fences, not to mention an abandoned bunker or two, questions arise quickly about this park's former use.

The U.S. government purchased this land from local residents and operated it as the Hingham Naval Depot Annex between 1941 and 1965. With the United States' involvement in World War II, arms production and military activity ramped up. Its use was revived again during the Korean War. This facility, commonly known as the Cohasset Annex, provided much ammunition to fuel the naval fleet of the Atlantic. A spur from the Old Colony Railroad led to this property. From the annex, tracks extended to the Hingham Naval Ammunition Depot at Bare Cove. The peak of its use was the year 1945. During that year, at the Cohasset Annex, over 2,000 nonmilitary personnel were employed, as well as over 700 sailors and officers and 375 Marine guards on site. Around 108 bunkers were located on the property. Most of them have been razed or filled in. The former train line from the park to the Old Colony Railroad has been reconditioned into a rail trail, known as the Whitney Spur, that connects Wompatuck State Park to the Cohasset commuter rail station.

It is not unusual to be wandering around the massive park of over 3,500 acres and stumble on a former military installation. The Commonwealth of Massachusetts took ownership of the land in 1966 after the U.S. Navy no longer had a use for it. From 1971 to 1982, the property was the home of the U.S. Army Reserve 187th Infantry Brigade. The most prominent and intriguing place in the park is Bunker N9. This bunker looked different from the rest in the park, but no one was quite certain what its use was. After it was discovered due to a cleanup by a Boy Scout group from Kingston, its history came to light. It contained the first nuclear depth charge created by the navy (yes, nuclear). A depth charge is a bomb used to blow up rival submarines. The bunker has extra layers of protection compared to most. Surface-to-air missiles were also built at this facility. Different races, both foot and bike, are held throughout the year at Wompatuck, including the appropriately named Landmine Bike Race—in an earlier day, venturing off course at this facility might have resulted in a detonated landmine.

The park is free of contaminants and offers a nifty perspective into the cycle of nature versus industry. The wilds that once inhabited this land were cleared for land by the settlers and then taken over by the heavy industry of the military, with nature winning out in the end, overtaking traces of its wartime past. Wompatuck is known for its array of flora and fauna, including the painted turtle, yellow warbler and mountain laurel. It is also the location of Prospect Hill, the highest point in all of Hingham. The visitor center at the park provides much needed orientation. Since the park is large, without an abundance of signage, it is important to stop there first or visit www.friendsofwompatuck.org online. The visitor center also includes the deed of the sale of Old Braintree from Chief Josiah Wompatuck to the English.

Bare Cove Park

Bare Cove Park Drive, Hingham, MA 02043
781-741-1400

While the Annex was mainly used for storage, the Hingham Naval Ammunitions Depot manufactured the ordnance used in the guns of the warships. The land that housed the depot was acquired by the navy from local residents in 1906. The first building campaign began five years later, as the area was used for Camp Hingham, which lasted until 1925. During that year, the camp structures, save for the depot, were demolished. The campus consisted of seventeen barracks, as well as a hospital, and was the training site for sailors. The depot was in full swing during the World War II years. Ships would stock up on munitions here en route to or from the Charlestown Navy Yard. Munitions were manufactured and supplied here. At the depot's peak in 1945, there were around 2,400 people here, more than some towns. The depot was its own self-sufficient community; it had a Howard Johnson's restaurant, a store, a pool, its own basketball team and a jazz band. Acclaimed saxophonist John Coltrane was stationed at Hingham and played in the band—a picture of the band with him in it can be viewed at the Hingham Naval Ammunition Depot Memorabilia Display at the Dock House. Although the base never saw any direct combat, a calamitous event took place in May 1944 when seventeen soldiers died. They were disposing of ammunition fifteen miles off the South Shore coast when an explosion ended their lives. The site also included underground bunkers and the Naval Handling Materials Laboratory, which directed how to pack cargo for ships all over the Atlantic. In all, there were roughly one hundred buildings on the campus. It lasted until 1961 and was decommissioned a year later. The navy kept control of the property until it was given to the Town of Hingham in 1971.

Bare Cove Park is located on 484 acres and flanked by the Weymouth Back River. The park is a wildlife sanctuary that contains a variety of flora and fauna. Similar to Wompatuck, remnants of the former military infrastructure still exist, with forlorn roads and decrepit piers echoing its former use. It is best known as being a popular spot for dog walking. Recently, a leash law was enacted at the park; prior to this, it was not uncommon to see herds of dogs off leash. Not all of the former property is Bare Cove Park. It also

These dock remnants at Bare Cove Park are among what remains of the property's former self. *Author's photo*.

consists of two museums, nearby condominium complexes and the South Shore Conservatory, an arts and music center. The conservatory building was once the commandant's house. On the Bare Cove property itself is the Dock House Museum; its contents include a variety of artifacts from its military use, including gas masks, many photographs and ammunition shells. The museum is operated by local firefighter Scott McMillan and holds open houses on a single Saturday during spring, summer and fall.

Also on the former site is the Bare Cove Fire Museum, which has been in existence since 1974. Its collection includes a variety of firetrucks and other apparatus, as well as much memorabilia. It is open Wednesday nights from seven to nine o'clock and is located at 45 Bare Cove Park Drive. Across the street is the South Shore Model Railroad Club and Museum. The group was founded in 1938 and moved to this site, a former warehouse for munitions, in 1998. They hold annual shows and open houses, which are available to the public. It is located at 52 Bare Cove Park Drive. Today, Bare Cove Park is another fascinating view of Hingham's military past. The park offers visitors a great place to walk the dog, ride a bike or go for a run. The coves of the Back River are gorgeous, with both land to explore and water views that encourage the visitor to stay awhile and escape the bombardment of modern life.

Webb Memorial State Park

371 River Street, North Weymouth, MA 02191
781-337-8624

This park, which is no longer an island, is considered part of the Boston Harbor Islands National Recreation Area. It became a state park in 1980—named in honor of Weymouth police captain and World War II veteran William Webb—and has a storied history from its days as seasonal grounds for Native Americans to a skirmish that occurred nearby during the Revolutionary War to its use as a Nike missile site in the mid-twentieth century. The park is located on a peninsula that juts out about a half mile into Hingham Bay on Weymouth's Back River, which separates the town from Hingham. Historically, this area of Weymouth, Weymouth Neck, was known as Wessagusset, the original settlement. Before landfill permanently connected it to the mainland, during high tide, what is now Webb Memorial was an island. Its primary use during the colonial days was as pastureland for grazing livestock. At the park, there is a marker in commemoration of the Grape Island Alarm (see next entry for more information), which took place on nearby Grape Island, also part of the Boston Harbor Islands, belonging to the Town of Weymouth.

The serenity of the grazing land ceased in the early 1860s when the Bradley Fertilizer Company turned Weymouth Neck/Fort Point into an industrial site. This was not just a factory; the sprawling complex consisted of many other components, including wharves, blacksmith shops and furnaces. The noxious mixture, which included parts of animals used in the fertilizer concoction, gave rise to the nickname Skunk Island. Industrial waste was dumped and buried in the ground. This was the largest plant of its kind in the world. There was a fire in 1946 that tore through the plant's acid tanks, and the inferno was so strong that nearby streets caught fire.

After its use as a fertilizer plant, the peninsula found new use as one of the many Nike antiaircraft missile sites in a network to protect Boston known as the Boston Defense Area. In Massachusetts, the defense system's sites were located in a ring around the city, similar to today's Route 95/128 belt. In all, there were twelve Nike sites situated in a ring around Boston from the North Shore to the South Shore. (Needham's Nike site was so predominant in the town that the high school mascot was and still is the Rockets.) The three-hundred-odd Nike sites were set up around the United

States to protect major civilian areas and assets during the Cold War. Each location consisted of two separate entities: the launch site, which stored the missiles underground; and the radar and tracking site. Here was the missile control center, where they would be fired. The Weymouth Neck site was also used to track incoming enemy jets. Nike missiles were defensive and could be steered via radar to explode an approaching bomber. The missiles were stored in Weymouth, with the control center located across Hingham Bay on what was called Little Hog Island and is now Spinnaker Island in Hull. (More about this island later.) The Nike site was also on the land adjacent to the park that is now the site of a complex of condominiums. Webb's tenure as a military holding ended in 1977, with it reconditioned into a state park three years later. Today, its former self is hidden from the public eye, as it is an enjoyable park for a stroll, observing nature or recreational activities and camping. It also affords the visitor spectacular skyline views of Boston. The park is located at 371 River Street in Weymouth, and although it is considered part of the Boston Harbor Islands, a boat is not needed to get there.

Fort Duvall–Little Hog Island

Spinnaker Island Causeway, Hull, MA 02045 (private)

This island was the location of the radar and control center for the Nike missile site across the bay, but the island's use for military function goes back further. Initially, this island was Fort Duvall, built in 1920 to protect Boston Harbor from attack. A practice shooting session in 1942 caused windows in buildings in nearby Hull to shatter. After World War II, the fort's use was ultimately eliminated, and it became part of the missile site in 1955. This lasted until 1974. Although the guns and fortification have been replaced by a complex of condominiums, the foundation of Fort Duvall can still be seen underneath the modern living spaces. It was renamed Spinnaker Island when the condominiums were built. The island is private, with a causeway connecting it to the tip of Hull's southern side. Prior to the roadway, the land mass was an actual island.

Hingham Shipyard

Shipyard Drive, Hingham, MA 02043

At the location of today's residential and commercial complex known as the Hingham Shipyard, there was an actual shipyard that produced 227 ships in three and a half years of existence. It was situated across the Weymouth Back River from the former Nike site and current Webb Memorial State Park. Before its use building ships, this section of land was the Bayside Airport, a small airfield which the military put to fast use as a shipbuilding center once the attack on Pearl Harbor signaled the United States' entrance into World War II. At the outset of the country's involvement, the fleet was outdated, with much of its apparatus dating from World War I. In what seemed like a moment's notice, the area was reconfigured to eventually employ twenty-three thousand individuals, many of whom were women, since much of the male workforce was active in the service. The contract was awarded to the Bethlehem Shipbuilding company, which was a branch of Bethlehem Steel from Pennsylvania. When the Pennsylvania-based company was granted the operation, its own shipyards were already full, so there was a need to create a new one. It was overseen by the nearby Fore River Shipyard in Quincy. The men and women of the South Shore who were to be employed here did not have the outright skills needed, so a group of a few hundred employees from Bethlehem had to train the workers. Train they did, as Hingham's production was top notch. The facility even won an award from the U.S. military—in 1943, the military commissioned sixty ships, but Hingham produced ninety. Talk about efficient. On-site, many destroyers and ships were

The Hingham Shipyard has been converted to a residential, shopping and eating destination, but the smokestack shows its former industrial past. *Jaclyn Lamothe.*

built, including the state-of-the-art destroyer *Escort*. Ships manufactured here were used in the pursuit and destruction of German U-boat submarines terrorizing the high seas. Among the craft built at the Hingham Shipyard were the landing ship tanks, amphibious vehicles that could be used both in the water and on the sand. These were used on beach attacks such as the Battle of Normandy. The creation of each ship was a cause for celebration, as the efforts at Hingham and other similar sites helped the Allied cause and were vital in winning the war. Shipbuilding here helped usher in a new dawn of a modern fleet of the American military.

Fore River Shipyard

Quincy, MA 02169

At one time, the Quincy shipyard employed the largest number of workers on the South Shore. During its one-hundred-year existence, the shipyard was operated by three different tenants: Thomas Watson in 1883 (of the Alexander Graham Bell "Watson, come here, I want to see you" fame), Bethlehem Steel in 1913 (later known as Bethlehem Shipbuilding Corporation) and General Dynamics in 1964. It had two offshoots in the South Shore: one in Hingham during the World War II years and the Victory Destroyer Plant in the Squantum section of Quincy from 1910 to 1920. This location today is known as Marina Bay, a community of residences and commercial businesses. An additional facility, the Bethlehem Atlantic Works, existed in East Boston. At the Fore River Shipyard, up to thousands of craft were manufactured, including destroyers, tankers and even submarines. Although closely associated with the construction of battleships, Fore River also built vessels for civilian use.

The shipyard initially began when Thomas Watson bought a sixty-acre farm in East Braintree. With his background in mechanics rather than agriculture, the farm was not successful. When his farm became a failure, he began investing in mechanics, specifically engines. The operation was known as Thomas Watson's Fore River Ship and Engine Company. The U.S. Navy first awarded the shipyard building contracts during the final years of the nineteenth century. The destroyers USS *Lawrence* and USS *Macdonough* were the last ships to be built here. The USS *Lawrence* was the first, from 1899 to 1900. In 1901, the company moved to Quincy Point, in the eastern portion of the town, on the banks of the Weymouth Fore River. The Fore

River Railroad was built in 1902. This was an extension of the Greenbush line to the shipyard. Throughout the shipyard's twentieth-century history, a number of strategic naval ships were manufactured here, including the USS *Massachusetts*, which launched in 1941 and is now displayed in the Taunton River as part of Battleship Cove in Fall River. The submarine the USS *Octopus* was built here and launched in 1906. It was commissioned by General Dynamics. Also built here during the 1940s was the USS *Salem*, a heavy cruiser currently docked at the site of the former shipyard as part of the United States Naval Shipbuilding Museum. A large schooner ship, the *Thomas W. Lawson*, was manufactured here; it would eventually meet its fate in a horrible wreck off the coast of England. Vessels were made here for the United Kingdom's Royal Navy, a battleship for the navy of Argentina and even submarines for the Japanese during the Russo-Japanese War. Later in the shipyard's tenure, large tankers and barges were built. In the World War II years, German U-boats were even known to clandestinely tail boats departing from the shipyard.

A bit of lore sprang up around the shipyard during the World War II years. The famous "Kilroy was here" graffiti that became part of the public consciousness may have originated here by an inspector and, later, Massachusetts state representative, James J. Kilroy. The bald-headed figure with a large proboscis peering over a ledge turned up in all corners of the country and even the world. Although some sources say that the Kilroy image predates James Kilroy, urban legend, be it truth or not, ensures that the "Kilroy was here" tag will be forever associated with the Fore River Shipyard.

Along with the construction of hundreds of ships was the inevitable increase in infrastructure. During the war years, the shipyard was at its height, with heavy numbers of commissioned projects from the military. A large steel mill was built on site during World War I. World War II saw the construction of the Hingham facility due to the quantity of workers needed. Postwar, the shift in manufacturing moved toward LNG (liquified natural gas) tankers and merchant ships in addition to the naval commissioned boats. The shipyard closed in 1963, with its acquisition by General Dynamics occurring a year later. Similar to many such facilities, a community sprang up around its plant. For instance, the workers at Fore River even fielded their own soccer team. At its height, the Fore River Shipyard employed around thirty-two thousand people. A ship was manufactured on average once every two weeks during this era. Building such immense vessels as tankers required the construction of the world's second-largest crane, known as the Goliath

Crane. The thirty-story mega-structure was completed in 1975 and used in the manufacture of LNG tankers. After the shipyard closed in 1986, Goliath remained a fixture of the Quincy coastline. It was disassembled in 2008. Tragically, in the process, ironworker Robert Harvey was killed. The crane was bought by a shipbuilding company out of South Korea for its facility in Romania, where it currently resides. The barge used to shuttle the pieces of the 328-foot crane was named in commemoration of the victim of the accident as the USS *Harvey.* Not only was the Fore River Shipyard the largest employer in the region, but it also aided in the defense of the United States for around one hundred years. It, along with the other facilities in the South Shore, all demonstrated how the military once played a tremendous role in its economy and its history. Today, the area where the shipbuilding operation once took place is still known as the Fore River Shipyard. Currently, it houses the U.S. Naval Shipbuilding Museum and USS *Salem.* More about the destroyer and museum follow. It has also made appearances in such Hollywood hits as *The Departed* and *The Company Men.*

USS Salem *and the United States Naval Shipbuilding Museum*

551 South Street, Quincy, MA 02169
617-479-7900, www.uss-salem.org, Admission $10

Located at the site of the Fore River Shipyard is the warship the USS *Salem,* which was built at this shipyard. The boat is docked here at least through 2021, as there has been talk that the ship will be docked somewhere else, possibly East Boston or Fall River, in the future. During the Halloween season, the ship is used as a "haunted battleship," creating a unique take on the traditional Halloween haunted house.

The USS *Salem* is classified as a heavy cruiser, which is a powerful warship that could hit targets that were far away and traveled at high rates of speed. It is the last of its kind still in existence. The boat is used as a museum today in commemoration of the service of the sailors and builders of the United States' naval effort. Exhibits at the museum include a tribute to sailors, model displays and presentations of the history of battleships. The boat itself is around 716 feet long. Its nickname is the "Sea Witch." The ship was built in the mid-1940s, launched in 1947 and used as the head warship in the United States' Mediterranean front during the Cold War. It was decommissioned in 1959 and kept in Philadelphia at the naval shipyard there. The Town of Quincy received the warship from the navy in 1992 as a token of appreciation for the years of shipbuilding history and importance in the town. Two years later, it docked at Quincy, and a year after that, the United States Naval Shipbuilding Museum was open. In recent years, the museum has been on the brink of closing. This is in part due to low attendance, as well as the wharf it was located at being deemed unsafe. (The ship moved to a more stable wharf.) The ship became a Hollywood star in the Massachusetts-based film *The Finest Hours*. Visit the website for more information about the ship as well as news about current events, renting it for birthday parties and even staying overnight on the boat.

Naval Air Station Squantum

Marina Bay: Victory Road, Quincy, MA 02171

A marshy tract of land known as the Squantum Peninsula, bordered by Quincy Bay and the Neponset River, became the site of the Harvard Aviation Field in 1910. It was leased from the New York, New Haven and Hartford Railroad by the Harvard Aeronautical Society. In 1916, the land was the site of the Hyde Park–based Sturtevant Aeroplane Company, which used the field for flight testing, as well as teaching the skill of flying. The navy took over the facility in 1917 at the outset of the United States' involvement in World War I. Here the field was used mainly as a facility for seaplanes and flight training. During the years of 1918 to 1920, the site was under the jurisdiction of the Fore River Shipyard. It was known as the Victory Destroyer Plant. Set on seventy acres, it employed roughly eight thousand workers and constructed thirty-five *Clemson*-class destroyers at the facility.

In 1923, this parcel of land was turned into the Naval Air Station Squantum. In existence until 1953, this was the first-ever naval reserve base. By the late 1920s, a small airfield was located here, with three large runways constructed between the years of 1939 and 1941. It was used as a training facility during World War II for the United States and the United Kingdom. Among the flight patrols based out of Squantum were those used to detect and attempt to destroy submarines. The most famous individual associated with Squantum was Ted Williams. Although he did not serve here, he did file his paperwork to become a civilian pilot. The land used by the navy included the former Dennison Airport. Amelia Earhart flew the first flight out of Dennison and was also an investor in the airport. Squantum was used for aviation training.

Squantum's peninsular geography made it difficult for takeoffs and landings. Compounding the problem was the rival air traffic from Logan Airport. This led to Squantum's closure, and its operations shifted to NAS South Weymouth. Today, this piece of land is Marina Bay, a complex of condominiums, restaurants and marinas. Also located here is Squantum Point Park, a picturesque locale with exquisite views of the Boston skyline and recreational paths for riding, walking and other similar activities. Prior to the opening of Marina Bay, whose development began in the 1980s, the area was the location of a research annex managed by the U.S. Air Force. After military use discontinued, the Boston Edison Company bought the land in hopes of building a nuclear power plant there. This never came to fruition, as the site settled on was eventually in the Manomet area of Plymouth and named the Pilgrim Nuclear Power Station. Today, Marina Bay comprises around two thousand residents, six restaurants and a 765-slip marina located at the former naval facility. Marina Bay is located around the area of Victory Road, and the Squantum Point Park is situated at the end of Miwra Haul Road, both in Quincy.

Naval Air Station South Weymouth

Union Point: 26 Memorial Grove Avenue, Weymouth, MA 02190
617-249-1105, www.unionpointma.com

The naval air station in Weymouth has close ties to its neighbor to the north, Squantum NAS. The land that turned into the air station was originally planned as a municipal airport. It launched as a naval facility in 1942 and closed its doors with the Base Realignment Act in 1997. Under the navy's jurisdiction, the first military use was as a blimp base; they were used to search for and destroy submarines during World War II. One blimp from the base met a mysterious demise off the coast of Bar Harbor. Officially, the accident—which killed six on board—was deemed due to human error. Many believe it was actually shot down by a German U-boat off the coast of Maine. After the war, Weymouth was used to store aircraft and then became an auxiliary landing field. By the early 1950s, rumblings of Squantum's closing became a reality. It closed in 1953, due to its peninsular location and proximity to Logan Airport. With the closure of the base, Weymouth was revamped and expanded from 1951 to 1953 so that larger aircraft could fit. Naval and marine reserves were stationed at the base. A special research-and-development team called the Naval Air Development Unit was also based here. This team's tenure ended in 1961, and so did the use of blimps in Weymouth. As the expansion of the facility continued in the 1950s, Union Street, which connected Rockland center to South Weymouth, was separated.

Since the base closed in 1997, much development and brouhaha have followed in its wake. First of all, the area was highly contaminated from the former infrastructure on site. This had to be remedied, with the navy footing the bill. It was then known as Southfield, which was primarily a development of mixed-use housing, with townhouses, single-family homes and an over-fifty-five facility, as well as commercial sites. There was talk of a movie studio that never came to fruition, although some of the abandoned base roads and runways have been the backdrop for sets in movies, including *Patriots Day*. The Southfield project grew, but not as swiftly as expected. A new developer took the reins, and the current plans are for Union Point, a modern "smart" city whose components are scheduled to include self-driving cars, a golf course, an MIT innovation center and major companies moving in. Union Point is named for the road that used to connect Rockland and Weymouth. There are already miles of nature trails for the public to enjoy. Also here is the Shea Field Aviation Historical Museum, which houses a collection of memorabilia such as photographs and artifacts from this base as well as the nearby Naval Air Station Squantum in Quincy. It is named for Jack Shea, who was stationed at Squantum and killed on the sinking of the USS *Wasp* during World War II by a Japanese submarine. Currently, the museum is looking for a permanent home. At the entrance to Union Point, on Shea Memorial Drive is a Douglas A-4 Skyhawk in tribute to the former use of the land.

Towers

Marshfield, Scituate and Plymouth

As part of Boston's waterfront defense system, a series of towers was built along the Massachusetts coastline from Plymouth to the North Shore. The most striking and accessible of these towers is the seventy-foot Brant Rock Tower, which looms above the seaside village of Brant Rock. This provided

180-degree viewing to spot enemy craft. Located farther north in Scituate is the Fourth Cliff Reservation. This complex, which is now utilized as a vacation spot for military families stationed at Hanscom Air Force Base, includes a five-story tower, two other towers and a tower that looks similar to a cottage, as well as a control bunker. Guns placed here protected the harbor during World War II. The gun foundations can still be seen. Fourth Cliff is inaccessible to the public, but for a view of the largest tower, ride through the residential neighborhoods of Bartletts Island (off of Bartletts Isle Way) or Trouant Island (accessible from Macombers Way). In Marshfield are remnants of the Holly Hill fire control radar. It is in a neighborhood close to Humarock; remnants remain, although it is now situated on private property. There was once a five-story concrete tower on Gurnet Point in Plymouth, which was Boston's most southern defense post. This has been razed. This tower was situated close to where the Plymouth Lighthouse is located. The best spot for viewing a former tower is visiting Brant Rock, since it is simply situated on the seawall and is accessible to the public for viewing it up close (although not inside).

The Forts of Plymouth

Accessed via Duxbury Beach (private road)

Plymouth had one of the first military installations in New England. A fort was a vital part of a defense system, and military life was intertwined with civilian life. (Case in point, the fort was also used as the first meetinghouse.) In more modern times, Plymouth has been the site of military installations. The fort, originally known as Gurnet Fort, was erected to protect the Plymouth Harbor during the American Revolution. During the war, the British fired shots at the fort and damaged the nearby lighthouse. It was reconstructed during the 1800s, eventually known as Fort Andrew and was discontinued in 1927. Also located in this area were a fire tower (mentioned earlier) and Fort Standish, built in 1863, which fell out of use by 1870 and was sold off in 1925. This was a Civil War–era fort constructed on Saquish Head. This earthen fort was equipped with canons, but it never saw action. It is now on private property. These forts are not accessible to the public.

Nike Sites

Hingham and Cohasset

As the Nike missile site in Weymouth and Hull protected the Boston area and the ammunitions base that is now Bare Cove Park in Hingham, the site at Hingham and Cohasset was in proximity to the ammunitions annex, current-day Wompatuck State Park. The outposts of Nike missile launching sites and control areas were erected for defensive measures in case of an attack by the Soviet Union during the Cold War. This former site, whose control center is located at today's Turkey Hill reservation, is managed by The Trustees, along with the Whitney and Thayer Woods, which is next to it. This Nike site lasted for five years, from 1956 to 1961. The only remnant is a concrete structure atop of Turkey Hill. The hope is to someday turn it into a museum about its history and that of others like it. The small size of the concrete structure is surprising. Benches are available to rest on inside. The launch site housed thirty missiles, located close by off of Route 3A in Cohasset at Crocker's Lane. The area today is where the Cohasset Sports Complex and Avalon Cohasset condominium complex are located. The land at Turkey Hill has been reclaimed by nature with preservation by The Trustees. It once held fields and stables and has reverted back to a nature preserve with around ten miles of trails and much flora and fauna protected on the property. There are two access points to Turkey Hill, one at the bottom of the hill on Route 3A, and the other near the top via the parking lot at the end of Turkey Hill Lane. The sixty-two-acre preserve came under management by The Trustees in 1997. Wompatuck State Park is connected to these properties as well.

Fort Revere–Hull

60 Farina Road Hull, MA 02045
www.fortrevere.org, Admission: Free

One of the more interesting places in the seaside village of Hull is Fort Revere. Hull's location literally jutting out into the ocean presented it as a prime spot for a fortification defending the area's major draw, Boston. Fort Revere protected Boston Harbor's south side, and Fort Heath in North Shore's Winthrop stood guard from the north.

Sitting atop what is known as Telegraph Hill are the remnants of the former Fort Revere, which stood witness to wartime throughout the history of America. Named after Paul Revere, a military armament of some kind stood on the spot from the days of the American Revolution up through World War II. Originally, this stronghold was named Fort Independence, but the name was later changed to honor local hero Paul Revere. The area was contemplated for military use as early as 1630, but Castle Island in today's South Boston was chosen instead. The first fort was built in 1776, and in 1827, the first telegraph tower was positioned there. The tower was used for signaling the entrance of ships into the harbor and knocked down in 1938. The fort consisted of a few gun installations, an officer's house, a fire tower and a water tower. Crews taking target and artillery practice led to a ruckus in town, not because of enemy fire, but from damage done to nearby homes and cottages. Luckily for history buffs, Fort Revere is still (partially) standing today, is (mostly) open and is free to visit. The public is allowed to explore the ins and outs of the fort, but be forewarned, it gets pretty dark in parts, especially in the tunnels and passageways. Unfortunately, given the fort's seemingly secluded location, it has become quite the hangout with partying teenagers. Do not be surprised to see empty beer cans, trash and walls containing graffiti.

Although the guns are gone, the gun mounts are still visible, so you will have to use your imagination when trying to spot a British enemy ship out at sea. Many of the bunkers still exist and can be climbed through. The most striking feature of the park is the 120-foot water tower on the premises. It was built in 1903 with the dual purpose of being a lookout tower as well. Its shape is reminiscent of a large obelisk and not a traditional water tower. Visitors were allowed to climb to the observation deck of the tower from 1975 to 2011, but due to safety concerns, access has been disallowed. Cracks are visible on the interior of the tower as well as the exterior. There also is a museum on the premises, but it has been discontinued due to danger. Although access to the observation deck and tower are no longer available, the fort's geographic location on top of a hill provides striking views of some of the Boston Harbor Islands, including Little and Great Brewster Island. The fort has even been used as a performance space for theatrical players since its discontinuation as a military facility.

Manomet Coast Guard Station

Manomet section of Plymouth, MA 02360

Located at the end of Manomet Point, high atop the hill overlooking dramatic cliffs that lead to the crashing Atlantic below, was once the Manomet Coast Guard Station, United States Coast Guard Station 31. This structure was built in 1874 and operational until 1947. It was razed in 1955. It was positioned near the iconic grand Mayflower Hotel here until a series of fires ravaged it, culminating in its 1975 demolition. Three brave heroes who were stationed here lost their lives on March 9, 1928. The steamship *Robert E. Lee* ran into trouble off the coast of Manomet, where it was caught on the Mary Ann Rocks. The Coast Guard had to assist with the rescue of passengers and crew. On the treacherous, stormy night in March, 3 guardsmen met their fate. All 273 on board the *Robert E. Lee* survived due to the historic feats of the Coast Guard. Behind the Lobster Pound on Manomet Point Road is a plaque detailing the tragic event and dedicated to the men. Bad luck continued to befall the SS *Robert E. Lee* when in 1942 it was torpedoed and sunk by a German U-boat in the Gulf of Mexico—25 of the over 400 passengers were killed.

Scituate Proving Grounds

Scituate, MA 02066, not accessible to the public

A military proving ground is an area where something new is tested, be it artillery, ordnance or strategic plans. Scituate was the location of a proving ground in 1918 and 1919. This parcel of land consisted of sixty-seven buildings of various uses, including storage of munitions, office work, laboratories and a power plant. Prior to the use by the military, it was privately owned land. Here gun carriages, including Howitzer carriages and Howitzer guns, were tested. They came from the arsenals at Watertown; Bridgeport, Connecticut; and Worcester. Howitzer carriages resemble small tanks. Around 140 men occupied the grounds of 115 acres. A spur of the Greenbush Railroad Line connected here, and a road ran from here to Boston and Watertown for ease of access. It was a military storage facility until 1921. When the military ceased using the proving grounds, it was the base for various operations, including moss processing. Moss was used in various household products.

Also located here was a very influential shortwave radio station, at one time the most powerful radio in the Western Hemisphere, operated by shortwave radio pioneer Walter S. Lemmon. During World War II, the station WRUL, or World Radio University Listeners, was known for powerful pro-democratic and anti-fascist broadcasts that could be heard as far away as Europe, Africa and Asia. Prior to the war effort, the station broadcast culturally relevant and academic programming. To combat the Nazis' use of browbeating propaganda, the station proclaimed to the world the benefits of democracy. The programs were broadcast in different languages, including Norwegian, and had a major influence on those abroad. The proving grounds were fitted with radio equipment, and antennas were scattered about the grounds. One segment included real New Englanders who were interviewed and told their stories of democracy to be broadcast to Europeans. It was a way to fight fascism without drawing a weapon. The station—along with the format—would change hands throughout the twentieth century. In 1966, its call letters changed to WNYW, which stood for "Radio New York Worldwide." The call letters were placed on the brick smokestack on the property.

The Glades/Strawberry Point

Glades Road, Scituate, MA 02066 (not accessible to the public)

On a peninsula in North Scituate, up the coast from Hatherly Beach, is a private gated community known as the Glades. At the Glades, or Strawberry Point, the U.S. government erected a series of fire towers to keep watch on Boston Harbor from 1940 to 1943. It consisted of two towers resembling cottages that survive today, two larger fire towers, a five-story and an eight-story tower and a one-hundred-foot radar tower. It was part of the larger Boston Harbor defense system. Public access is denied to this site.

Point Allerton Coast Guard Station

1117 Nantasket Avenue, Hull, MA 02045
781-925-5433, www.lifesavingmuseum.org, Admission: $5

The Coast Guard Point Allerton Station is world renowned in terms of lifesaving facilities. Point Allerton is now a museum known as the Hull

Lifesaving Museum. Point Allerton, built in 1889, is the third oldest of its kind in the world. The architect of the green and red Queen Anne–style building was Albert Bibb. It housed the Massachusetts Humane Society, a precursor to the Coast Guard. It officially became a possession of the Coast Guard in 1915. Captain Joshua James oversaw operations here. A famed lifesaver, he and his crew hold the claim of saving over one thousand lives. Given Hull's position guarding Boston Harbor, the Coast Guard had its work cut out for itself, with the numerous shipwrecks and other accidents stranding folks at sea. The museum features exhibits on the maritime history of Boston Harbor, artifacts pertaining to the lifesaving station and a research library. It also offers events throughout the year such as Harbor Illumination, a rowing program and a lecture series.

The current Coast Guard Facility in Hull is located on Highland Avenue, near the corner with Main Street. The Scituate Coast Guard Station is operated by the Hull branch and is open seasonally. It is located on the road adjacent to Front Street, next to the parking lots used for the businesses at Scituate Harbor. This area was on the forefront of lifesaving services, as the first lifeboat was built in Cohasset in 1807. Massachusetts Humane Society Station 23 was located in Cohasset at Pleasant Beach on Atlantic Avenue. The former boathouse is now in the possession of the Scituate Historical Society and is located on Edward Foster Road, utilized by the Scituate Recreation Department.

Plymouth Auxiliary Airport

246 South Meadow Road, Plymouth, MA 02060
508-746-2020, www.pymairport.com

Plymouth's aviation history began in 1934, when Edward Griffith cleared some of his land to create the first runway. Throughout the 1930s, the airport was used for mail flights to Boston, biplane flights and even a short-lived airplane company known as Mayflower Airlines, which operated here in 1936. During World War II, the government was acquiring airfields for military use. In 1942, the navy purchased the airport and erected barracks and a hangar. It was primarily used for training purposes. Most of the flyers out of Plymouth were American, but the roster included some men from New Zealand and Australia. The Plymouth airport was an outlying airfield in conjunction with the Squantum base in Quincy. After the war effort was over, Plymouth retained the field. The navy sold it to the town for one dollar. Today, it is used for private airplanes, aviation apparatus of the state police, plane mechanics associated with a nearby community college and flying lessons. The Alpha One Flight School airplane hangar is a holdover from its naval days. It is also the site of Plane Jane's restaurant, open for breakfast and lunch.

National Fireworks Property/Pilgrim Ordnance Works

Accessible via King Street, Hanover, MA 02340

Buried deep in suburban Hanover, close to the borders shared with Hanson and Pembroke, is the National Fireworks Property, which was the site of a former forge that manufactured cannons used in the American Revolution. In the early twentieth century, the property became the possession of the National Fireworks Company. In addition to civilian fireworks such as cherry bombs and firecrackers, the company also produced munitions and explosives for the military. There were storage and testing areas on the property. Before the establishment of the fireworks factory, this property housed, at various times, a mill, a foundry and a tack factory. The fireworks site was massive, with dozens of buildings. It manufactured explosives for the military from World War I up to 1970. An explosion in 1967 killed an employee, injured many others and ripped the roof and backside off a building when an antipersonnel mine used in the Vietnam War fell from a shelf onto the floor. Close to the property off Plain Street was the Pilgrim Ordnance Works. During World War II it was a magnesium plant, operated by the National Fireworks Company, as well as a holding cell for prisoners of war. Part of this parcel of land is now the Plain Street Site, a green space owned by the Town of Hanover, which offers visitor trails on the former site roads. It is located behind residential neighborhoods, but one access point is via the end of Bailey Road. As of the time of writing, there is no signage, simply a path in the woods at the end of the cul-de-sac.

The former National Fireworks Company property is also part of Hanover's public land. There has been much environmental concern. Although the site closed over forty years ago, live ordnance has been located. Most of it is in the lower portion of the property and is fenced off, although other places have been found to be active. The cleanup of this area was in the works for years, but as recently as 2017 and 2018, controlled munitions blasts have occurred here. Factory Pond, as of this writing, has high levels of contaminants from the explosives site. Buildings that are in various states of disrepair are scattered throughout the property. Despite the controversy, the park does contain over four miles of kept up trails. It has an access point on King Street. Look for the small parking lot and sign marking the entrance.

Fort Andrews—Peddocks Island

Part of the Boston Harbor Islands, Hull, MA 02045

Peddocks Island, one of the Boston Harbor Islands, is located right near the tip of the Hull peninsula. Today, it is accessible by ferry, and camping overnight is allowed. One of the largest forts that protected Boston Harbor was Fort Andrews. At one time, there were roughly thirty structures on the property, including large residences and a hospital. Some buildings still remain, others have been destroyed and others partially remain in a state of decay. There have been talks of rehabilitating some to be turned into a museum. The Martin Scorsese film based on local author Dennis Lehane's book *Shutter Island* was partially filmed among the remnants of the fort. There were a series of World War II–era fire-control towers on the island and atop Point Allerton. The fort had been shuttered by the mid-twentieth century.

BIBLIOGRAPHY

Books and Articles

Adams, Charles Francis. *History of Braintree, Massachusetts: The North Precinct of Braintree, And the Town of Quincy.* Cambridge, MA: Riverside Press, 1891.

Alden, Timothy. *A Collection of American Epitaphs and Inscriptions with Occasional Notes Volume 3.* New York: S. Marks, 1814.

Anonymous. *Boot and Shoe Recorder: The Magazine of Fashion Footwear, Volume 81, Part 2.* Charleston, SC: Nabu Press, 2011.

Bailey, Sarah Y. *The Story of Jones River in Pilgrim Plymouth, 1620–1726.* Kingston, MA: Kingston Branch of the Alliance of Unitarian Women, 1920.

Baker, Ed. "River Herring Are Back in East Weymouth with Impressive Numbers." Wicked Local Weymouth. April 25, 2016. weymouth.wickedlocal.com.

Baker, Guy S. *History of Halifax, Massachusetts.* Madison: University of Wisconsin–Madison, 1976.

Baker, James W., and Jonathan W. Keith. *Plymouth Through Time.* Gloucestershire, UK: Fonthill Media, 2013.

Bates, Torey. *The Shoe Industry of Weymouth.* Weymouth, MA: Weymouth Historical Society, 1933.

Bolton, Michele Morgan. "Former Fireworks Site Cleanup Stalled." *Boston Globe,* June 30, 2011.

Boston Globe. "New England Broadcasts to Tell Europe of Democracy." August 18, 1948.

Bradford, William. *Of Plymouth Plantation: 1620–1647.* Boston: McGraw-Hill, 1981.

Braithwaite, Nancy. "The History of the Marshfield Historical Society." Marshfield Historical Society, marshfieldhistoricalsociety.com.

Brechlin, Earl. "Fate of K-14: Blimp Hits the Water; Six Men Perish." *Ellsworth American,* January 13, 2012.

Brewster, Ellis W. *Plymouth in my Father's Time.* Plymouth, MA: Pilgrim Society, 1968.

Briggs, Lloyd Vernon. *History of Shipbuilding on North River, Plymouth County, Massachusetts: With Genealogies of the Shipbuilders and Accounts of the Industries Upon Its Tributaries, 1642 to 1872.* Plymouth County, MA: Coburn Brothers, 1889.

Burbank, Alfred Stevens. *Guide to Historic Plymouth.* Ann Arbor: University of Michigan Library, 1917.

Burrows, Brittany. "What's Happening Here?: The Most Famous Legs in Town." *Wicked Local*, March 22, 2011. www.wickedlocal.com.

Butterfield, Fox. "The Perfect New England Village." *New York Times*, May 14, 1989.

Cameron, Dr. James R. "Solomon Willard." *Quincy History* no. 29 (Spring 1993).

Cann, Donald, and John Galluzzo. *Rockland.* Charleston, SC: Arcadia Publishing, 2003.

Carll, Adam Ignatius. "History of Wompatuck." Friends of Wompatuck, friendsofwompatuck.org.

Cavallo, Orlando N., Jr. *Pembroke Herring Run: A History of the Valley and History.* Pembroke, MA: Brown Printing Services, n.d.

Cheney, Glenn Alan. *Thanksgiving.* New London, CT: New London Librarium, 2013.

The Committee for Preservation of Hull's History. *Hull & Nantasket Beach.* Charleston, SC: Arcadia Publishing, 1999.

Cornish, Louis C. *The History of Hingham, Massachusetts.* Boston: Churchill and Rockwell, 1911.

Cotter, Sean Philip. "40 Years in the Making, Marina Bay Comes of Age." *Patriot Ledger*, February 16, 2018.

Crowell, Margaret. "Along the North River: Stream of Indian Canoes, Pioneer Ships and Modern Craft Described." *Hanover Branch and Norwell Advertiser.* Souvenir Supplement for Norwell, MA, Seventh Annual Edition, May 27, 1938.

Davis, William T. *Ancient Landmarks of Plymouth.* Boston: Damrell & Upham, 1899.

———. *Plymouth Memories of an Octogenarian.* Plymouth, MA: Memorial Press, 1906.

Deetz, James. *In Small Things Forgotten: An Archaeology of Early American Life.* New York City: Anchor, 1996.

Doucette, Dianna. *Annasnappet Pond: 9000 Years in Carver, MA, Archeology for the Route 44 Reconstruction Project.* Pawtucket, RI: Public Archeology Laboratory Inc., 1997.

Dwyer, Dialynn. "A Swastika Replaced by an American Flag." Boston.com. July 1, 2015. www.boston.com.

Eaton, Walter Prichard. *Plymouth—1620.* New Haven, CT: New York, New Haven and Hartford Railroad Company, 1928.

Flint, E. Willard, ed. *National Fireworks Review.* Philadelphia: Edward Stern & Company, 1944.

Ford, Elise. "A Piece of the Rockwell." *Washington Post*, December 14, 1994.

Ford, Mary. "Former NIKE Missile Base Building in Cohasset Could be Restored." *Cohasset Mariner*, March 2, 2018.

Franklin, Abigail E. *Mills and Muskrats on the Monatiquot—The Story of Braintree's River.* Braintree, MA: Braintree Historical Society, 2003.

Frattasio, Marc J. *NAS Squantum: The First Naval Air Reserve Base.* N.p.: self-published, 2013.

Furlong, C. Wellington. "Land of the Men of Kent." Scituate Historical Society. scituatehistoricalsociety.org.

Gallerani, Kathryn. "Luminaries: Main Street at Christmas." *Kingston Wicked Local*, December 17, 2014. kingston.wickedlocal.com.

Galluzzo, John. "Classic Cookie Creators." *South Shore Living*, November 2011.

———. "Hanover's Four Corners," *South Shore Living*, November 2017.

Goldstein, Karin. "Spring Street: A Path Through History." *Patch—Plymouth*, May 14, 2011. patch.com.

———. "A Street from Yesteryear." *Patch—Plymouth*, January 11, 2012. patch.com.

Goodwin, John Abbot. *The Pilgrim Republic: An Historical Review of the Colony of New Plymouth, with Sketches of the Rise of Other New England Settlements, the History of Congregationalism and the Creeds of the Period.* Boston: Houghton, 1899.

Griffith, Henry S. *History of the Town of Carver, Massachusetts: Historical Review, 1637 to 1910.* New Bedford, MA: E. Anthony & Sons, 1913.

Gural, Harry, Peg Charlton and Jess Cain. *Remembering the Hingham Shipyard.* DVD. Boston: Powderhouse Productions, 2000.

Hamilton, Neil A. *The 1970s—Eyewitness History.* New York: Facts on File, 2006.

Harbert, Rich. "Five Centuries on Long Beach." *Wicked Local—Plymouth*, September 7, 2010. www.wickedlocal.com.

Hayes, Karen. "Oliveira's." *Boston Globe*, September 2, 2001.

Heath, Dwight, ed. *Mourt's Relation: A Journal of the Pilgrims at Plymouth.* New York: Corinth Books, 1963.

Heinrichs, Mary. *Weymouth History.* WETC-8, www.weymouth.ma.us.

Hickey, David. *Whitman.* Charleston, SC: Arcadia Publishing, 2003.

Hingham: A Story of Its Early Settlement and Life, Its Ancient Landmarks, Its Historic Sites and Buildings. Hingham, MA: Old Colony Chapter, Daughters of the American Revolution, 1911.

Hobart, Benjamin. *History of the Town of Abington: Plymouth County, MA—From Its First Settlement.* Boston; T.H. Carter and Son, 1866.

Holly, H. Hobart. *Quincy History.* Publication of the Quincy Historical Society, no. 27 (Spring 1992).

Howe, Henry F. *Early Explorers of Plymouth Harbor, 1525–1619.* Plymouth, MA: Plimoth Plantation and Pilgrim Society, 1953.

Howe, Oliver H. *A Brief Sketch of the History of Cohasset.* Cohasset, MA: Cohasset Historical Society, 1941.

Huiginn, Eugene Joseph Vincent. *The Graves of Myles Standish and Other Pilgrims.* Boonville, NY: Herald and Tourist Steam Print, 1892.

Hurd, D. Hamilton, ed. *History of Plymouth County, Massachusetts, with Biographical Sketches of Many of Its Pioneers and Prominent Men, Part 1.* Philadelphia, PA: J.W. Lewis & Company, 1884.

Hurwitz, Eric. *Massachusetts Town Greens: A History of the State's Common Centers.* Lanham, MD: Rowan and Littlefield, 2016.

Jackman, Bob. "Marshfield Commentary: More Dike History Flows In." *Marshfield Mariner*, May 26, 2012.

Johnson, Carolyn Y. "From Brant Rock Tower, Radio Age Was Sparked." *Boston Globe,* July 30, 2006.

Kingsport News. "Explosives Plant Blast Kills One." December 28, 1967.

Klein, Christopher. *Discovering the Boston Harbor Islands.* Boston: Union Park Press, 2011.

Knox, Robert. "Fires Down Below." *Boston Globe,* July 17, 2011.

Krusell, Cynthia Hagar, and Betty Magoun Bates. *Marshfield: A Town of Villages, 1640– 1990.* Marshfield, MA: Historical Research Associates, 1990.

Krusell, Cynthia Hagar, and John J. Galluzzo. *Marshfield.* Charleston, SC: Arcadia Publishing, 2007.

LaCrosse, Mike. "Hanover Pond Closed After Fisherman Hooks Explosive Device." WBZ News, June 16, 2018. boston.cbslocal.com.

Lambert, Lane. "Obama's Roots Trace Back to Plymouth and New World's Earliest Settlers." Wicked Local—Plymouth, January 18, 2009. www.wickedlocal.com.

Lincoln Jr., Solomon. *History of the Town of Hingham, Plymouth County, Massachusetts.* Hingham, MA: C. Gill Jr., 1927.

Littlefield, Cyril O. *Reminiscences and Facts on Mayflower Grove, Bryantville, in the Town of Pembroke, Massachusetts, 1901–1940.* Pembroke, MA: Pembroke Historical Society, 1975.

Lovett, Rachel. "Then and Now: The South Hanover Fire Station." Wicked Local Hanover, April 15, 2016. hanover.wickedlocal.com.

Maas, Steve. "A Modest Museum Bears Testimony to Key Ammo Depot During WWII." *Boston Globe,* August 22, 2013.

Maggio, John. *The Italian Americans.* PBS. DVD, 2015.

Markman, Joseph. "Scout Hopes to Reclaim Whitman Railroad History." *The Enterprise,* April 14, 2014.

Moore, Vanessa. "As Strong as Metal and Stone: Meet the Monumental Women of Plymouth." *The Spectrum,* Spring 2018.

Movementum Realty. *The Everything Duxbury Guide.* N.p., 2017.

Murphy, Meg. "Remembering Eleanor Norris and the Land She Loved." *Boston Globe,* January 17, 2013.

Nash, Gilbert. *Historical Sketch of the Town of Weymouth, Massachusetts: From 1622 to 1884.* Weymouth, MA: Weymouth Historical Society, 1885.

National Balloon Museum. "Hall of Fame: Ben Abruzzo." www. nationalballoonmuseum.com.

New York Times. "Boston Steamer Wrecked in Storm." March 10, 1928.

Norwell Historical Society. *Discussion on the Assinippi/Jacobs Lane Area of Norwell.* N.p., n.d.

Norwell Historical Society and Norwell Cemetery Commission. *Historic Cemeteries in Norwell.* N.p., n.d.

Old Scituate. Scituate, MA: Chief Justice Cushing Chapter, Daughters of the American Revolution, 1921.

Olson, Samuel H. *A Narrative of South Scituate & Norwell 1849–1963: Remembering Its Past and the World Around It.* Charleston, SC: The History Press, 2010.

Peabody, Robert E. *The Derbys of Salem, Massachusetts: A Study of Eighteenth-Century Commerce Carried on by a Family of Typical New England Merchants.* Salem, MA: Essex Institute, 1908.

Perkins, Frank H. *Handbook of Old Burial Hill—Plymouth, Massachusetts: Its History, Its Famous Dead and Its Quaint Epitaphs.* Plymouth, MA: A.S. Burbank, 1902.

Peters, Sharon Orcutt. *Abington.* Charleston, SC: Arcadia Publishing, 2002.

Philbrick, Nathaniel. *Mayflower: A Story of Courage, Community and War.* New York: Viking, 2006.

Plympton Historical Commission. *Self Guided Walking Tour of the Plympton Historic District.* N.p., n.d.

Porter-Brown, Nell. "Sweet Sweat," *Harvard Magazine.* July–August 2016.

Proctor, Karen. "Kingston's Past—Jones River Figured Keenly in Shipbuilding Days." *Kingston Wicked Local*, April 5, 2007.

———. *Pembroke.* Charleston, SC: Arcadia Publishing, 2008.

Richards, Lysander Salmon. *History of Marshfield Volume 1.* Charleston, SC: Nabu Press, 2010.

Ronan, Patrick. "USS Salem Will Stay in Quincy Through 2020." *Patriot Ledger*, February 23, 2016.

SAILS Digital History Collections. "History of the Town of Hanson." http://sailsinc.omeka.net/items/show1016.

Sarcone, Anthony F., and Lawrence S. Rines. *A History of Shipbuilding at Fore River.* Quincy, MA: Quincy Junior College, Department of History, 1975.

Sparks, Hannah. "Historians Hope to Recount Great Brant Rock Fire for 75th Anniversary." *Marshfield Mariner*, April 28, 2016.

Strong, Warren P., ed. *The Wharves of Plymouth.* Plymouth, MA: Pilgrim Hall, 1955.

Sweeney, Emily. "The Last of the Tramp Houses." *Boston Globe*, June 5, 2014.

Tolles, Bryant F. *Summer by the Seaside: The Architecture of New England Coast Resort Hotels, 1820–1950.* Chicago: University of Chicago Press, 2008.

Triant, Diane Speare. "Stoical 25-Year-Old Reminder of the Honor Due First People." *Boston Globe*, August 24, 2008.

Tucker, Norman P. *Kingston.* Charleston, SC: Arcadia Publishing, 2001.

Twelley, Jedediah, and John F. Simmons. *History of the Town of Hanover with Family Genealogies.* Hanover, MA: Town of Hanover, 1920.

Wade, Herbert T. *Handbook of Ordnance Data.* Washington, DC: Government Print Office, 1919.

Wadsworth, David H., Paula Morse and Lynne DeGiacomo. *Cohasset.* Charleston, SC: Arcadia Publishing, 2004

Weimer, Adrian Chastain. *Martyr's Mirror: Persecution and Holiness in Early New England.* Oxford: Oxford University Press, 2014.

Werny, Frank. *Walks Among the Pines and Ponds of Plymouth and Surrounding Areas: Easy Hikes in and around the Plymouth, MA Area.* Scotts Valley, CA: CreateSpace, 2009.

White, Thomas, Jr., and Samuel White. *Ancestral Chronological Record of the William White Family from 1607–08 to 1895.* Concord, MA: Republican Press Association, 1895.

Wicked Local Carver. "Visit Myles Standish Monument in Duxbury." August 13, 2018. carver.wickedlocal.com.

Wyman, Carolyn. *The Great American Chocolate Chip Cookie Book: Scrumptious Recipes & Fabled History from Toll House to Cookie Cake Pie.* Woodstock, VT: Countryman Press, 2013.

Websites

Websites for the town, the attraction or historical society were referenced.

A special thanks to the following individuals for their expertise:

Carol Anderson, Kingston
Kezia Bacon, Marshfield
James Baker, Plymouth
Wendy Bawabe and Caleb Estabrooks, Norwell
Tom Begley, Plimoth Plantation
Lynne DeGiacomo, Cohasset
Bob Gallagher, Scituate
Miles Prescott, Pembroke
Samantha Woods, the Herring Run

INDEX

ABOUT THE AUTHOR

Originally from Connecticut, Zack Lamothe earned a degree in American studies at Boston University. He has lived on the South Shore since 2011. He is author of *Connecticut Lore: Strange, Off Kilter and Full of Surprises* and the sequel, *More Connecticut Lore: Guidebook to 82 Strange Locations*. Lamothe is a monthly contributor to *Norwich Magazine* and writes for other various print and online publications. He manages and writes for the travel website www.backyardroadtrips.com. He teaches in Marshfield and lives in Plymouth with his wife, two kids and their dog, Pepper.